# Minimalism and Decluttering:

## *The Easier Way of Life as a Minimalist. 11 Simple Steps to Declutter Your Life from a Useless Stuff and Supercharge Your Life!*

# Table Of Contents

Introduction..............................................6

Chapter 1 Minimalism Meets Decluttering...............................................7

Chapter 2 Perks of Minimalism and Decluttering, According to Science.........13

Chapter 3 Signs and Symptoms of a Cluttered Life............................................20

Chapter 4 A Minimalist Guide to Immediately Decluttering Your Life......28

Chapter 5 Creating a Minimalist and Decluttered Home...................................40

Chapter 6 Going Minimal With Social Media..........................................................97

Chapter 7 Guide to Financial Minimalism.............................................105

Chapter 8 Embracing the Minimalist Diet............................................................116

Chapter 9 Adopting a Minimalist and Clutter-Free Wardrobe.........................137

**Chapter 10 Mastering The Art of
Minimalist Traveling**............................154

**Chapter 11 Saving the Environment by
Living Minimally**..................................167

**Conclusion**..............................................179

© **Copyright 2019 by Ryan Martinez - All rights reserved.**

The content contained within this book may not be reproduced, duplicated or transmitted without direct written permission from the author or the publisher.

Under no circumstances will any blame or legal responsibility be held against the publisher, or author, for any damages, reparation, or monetary loss due to the information contained within this book, either directly or indirectly.

Legal Notice:

This book is copyright protected. It is only for personal use. You cannot amend, distribute, sell, use, quote or paraphrase any part, or the content within this book, without the consent of the author or publisher.

Disclaimer Notice:

Please note the information contained within this document is for educational and entertainment purposes only. All effort has been executed to present accurate, up to date, reliable, complete information. No warranties of any kind are declared or implied. Readers acknowledge that the author is not engaging in the rendering of legal, financial, medical or professional advice. The content within this book has been derived from various sources. Please consult a licensed professional before attempting any techniques outlined in this book.

By reading this document, the reader agrees that under no circumstances is the author responsible for any losses, direct or indirect, that are incurred as a result of the use of information contained within this document, including, but not limited to, errors, omissions, or inaccuracies.

# Introduction

This book contains everything you need to live life without feeling like you are constantly chasing after something, and trying so hard to possess one material thing after another, that you longer appreciate all the good things you do have and you forget to actually enjoy what the world around you has to offer at no extra cost.

This book will help you to reclaim the clutter-free, relaxing, elegant, simplified, and livable state of your home while also taking care of the environment; to live your life in the moment and go off on adventures around the world instead of being tied to your phone; and to use your money wisely in financing your need for healthy food and sensible clothing as well as your desire to travel and gain experiences.

Reading this book will give you the minimalism and decluttering know-how it takes to change your life for the better.

Thanks for purchasing this book, I hope you enjoy it!

# Chapter 1 Minimalism Meets Decluttering

Decluttering, Decoded

Decluttering is the resulting action you take for wanting to clear out your bedroom drawers, your entire home, your work schedule, your mental space, or all aspects of your life. You may need to relocate to another city, wish to consolidate your possessions after getting married, or simply let go of belongings that you no longer find useful.

Decluttering can also arise from a shift in your perspective in life – a loved one may have recently passed and you realize that the things he or she had left behind are not necessarily the things you would want to keep for yourself or even pass on to your kids. It can even be the result of your being overwhelmed by the large number of belongings that are holding you back from living your life to the fullest.

You might think decluttering is something you perform as a one-time, big-time activity that simply involves getting rid of barely worn clothes and other dispensable stuff. But the truth is that you do a one-big-purge only if you make sure to maintain decluttering in your life.

Road to Minimalism

The good news is that the act of constantly decluttering will help steer you toward learning about and practicing minimalism. You will observe within yourself a significant shift in how you perceive each aspect of your life. You start noticing how more at peace you feel at home since you deliberately kept clutter from creeping onto surfaces and into corners. You learn to appreciate how effortless it is for you to throw on an outfit every single morning and know that you look great in it.

Decluttering makes you feel like breathing much easier, knowing that your list of activities for the day consists only of essential tasks. It helps you figure out that you only need simple things to feed your body so that you look and feel confident in your own skin. Decluttering also allows you to let go of unnecessary things that clutter your mind and fill it instead with clarity. Ultimately, you discover the beauty in having less in order to live more. You start seeing the joy in not having to fill your home with all kinds of trinkets, your time with uncalled-for commitments, and your mind with pointless thoughts.

In the end, decluttering leads you to practicing minimalism in your life.

You are living in a world that is constantly enticing you to want to have more, which eggs you on to buy more. Advertisements come at you and make you believe you will only feel satisfied with yourself if you keep getting more stuff. But every purchase actually makes you feel more mentally and emotionally loaded, eventually causing you to lose the freedom to spend time on the things that actually matter to you and that bring value and fulfillment to your life.

Slave No More

Minimalism enables you to get rid of the things you do not need in your life. It helps you see the sensibility in giving up those worthless knickknacks you have been storing in your treasure chest all these years. It allows you to reclaim valuable spaces that you can fill with stuff that you truly need to live your life to the fullest.

Practicing the minimalist lifestyle helps you remember that you become a slave to the material things that you get attached to. You end up wasting precious time cleaning and organizing all the things you have accumulated, time that you could have used in pursuing our passions and realizing your goals. This is the reason a minimalist feels happy when he sees his cabinets and drawers are empty – it means he has eliminated the stuff that do not help him achieve his dreams.

No Strings Attached

Minimalism helps you let go of being attached to your possessions, which is a big reason you find it difficult to throw away stuff. This is especially true for things that make you remember particular times or experiences in your life. But living the minimalist way reminds you of the fact that your mind holds the memories that you share with family and friends, not your belongings. Minimalism helps you realize that, instead of dwelling in the past, you are better off looking forward to what the future holds for you. Rather than forming an attachment to your treasures and trinkets, you should be forming bonds with people.

Order In the Court

Being a minimalist drives home why it makes sense to keep your home decluttered and organized. It helps you see the importance of making sure each item you own has a specific use as well as a particular space to store it. Everything becomes easier when you know where something is every single time because you keep it one place only.

Sitting Un-Pretty No More

Minimally is extremely helpful when it comes to curbing your spending. It teaches you to always purchase things with care to avoid buying anything that do not serve a purpose or add value to your life. Minimalism also something has to go each time you buy new stuff and bring it into your home. Things you will have to let go, either by donating or selling, includes those that simply sit and gather dust.

Life, Simplified

Because minimalism promotes getting rid of material things that are not necessary in your life, it encourages you to also:

• Lean towards digitization: Enjoy the convenience of scanning photos into a memory drive or a computer, then throwing away the photos themselves. You can also make use of technology in creating photo albums, letters, tickets, and invoices.

• Multitask with technology: You can still accomplish all the things you need to do without having to use a desktop computer, a laptop, a tablet, a cellphone, and a music player. You can definitely make do with just one or two devices.

- Limit information consumption: With you getting exposed to floods of stimulation all through your day, it is no wonder why you end up losing focus on the information you should truly care about. Minimalism helps you avoid becoming lost in the world of consumerism and being updated on the important stuff going on across the globe instead.

- Prioritize your commitments: Adopting the minimalist lifestyle steers you towards accomplishing more things by using your time wisely, rather than wasting it unproductive meetings or dates. It helps you learn simply refuse to do or participate in something if you know it would not be of value to you.

- Place emphasis on experiences: Minimalism helps you see the joy in having more experiences instead of material possessions.

- Take charge of your thoughts: Living the minimalist way makes you see the significance of controlling your mind and concentrating on the things that truly matter to you as you strive for emotional balance as well.

# Chapter 2 Perks of Minimalism and Decluttering, According to Science

Science reveals that accumulating more stuff in your life does not guarantee you happiness. A study done in 2017 determined that clutter is closely linked to procrastination, with people opting not to clear out their homes because they find it cleaning and organizing too much of a burden. The problem is that avoiding household work actually has a negative impact on your mind's well-being. The same study reported that having problems with clutter resulted to an increase in feelings of dissatisfaction among older adults.

Living with clutter, according to another study, also raises your cortisol (stress hormone) levels. It was found that women in cluttered homes had increased cortisol levels all through the day. The same women also disclosed that, as the day progressed, they felt more depressed, and that on top of finding it hard to make the transition from work life to home life, they felt more tired when evening came. Men showed less signs of being bothered by clutter, which explains their lower cortisol levels. With such results, the study suggests the higher sense of responsibility that women have for their home environments, in contrast to men.

Your concentration can also be negatively affected by living in a cluttered home. A Princeton Neuroscience Institute study revealed that being exposed to high levels of visual stimuli prevents the brain from properly focusing and processing information. This is the reason people's mental power and productivity level dip when looking at too many things at the same time.

Benefits of Minimalism and Decluttering

Eliminating clutter from your life can be overwhelming, but you will be reaping plenty of benefits out of it:

Better sleep: If you have ever experienced lying in bed and getting stressed out from staring at either your cluttered closet or towering laundry pile in the hamper, then you must also have experienced hardly getting any rest. A recent study on sleep found a link between lacking sleep and a messy room, especially if the person involved is highly likely to develop a hoarding disorder. The sleeping problem may involve finding it difficult to fall asleep at nighttime and having trouble going back to sleep when awakened.

More focus on goals: Allowing clutter to accumulate means you will be constantly reminded of all the stuff you had to do but failed to follow through. While such a situation may be good in the beginning, such as a yoga mat standing in a corner helps you remember to finally start your stretching routine, it can later on lead to the yoga mat going unused for months until it becomes a form of clutter. Your reason for keeping stuff and living with all that mess could be that you are sure you will finally lose that extra twenty pounds and actually fit into your favorite jeans, or you just know that you will find the time to read all of those old newspapers stacked on the living room floor. But the truth is that those things that you do not really need but are still holding onto will only serve as symbols of guilt and shame instead of being your objects for motivation and inspiration.

Intensified concentration: Having a mess on your home office desk can make getting anything done an absolutely painful chore. But it may surprise you to know that taking the time to get rid of those unnecessary papers and then returning everything you do need in an organized manner can help you get started on your work almost right away. It does not even matter if you are going to be working with an office desk or your bedroom close. Being surrounded by too many things can negatively affect your focusing and information processing ability. A Princeton University study showed that people's task performances differ depending on whether they are working in an organized or a cluttered space. The same study also revealed that when your surroundings have physical clutter, the latter ends up competing for your attention and causes your stress levels to increase and your performance level to go down. Basically, useless stuff only leads your brain to do multitasking, and therefore eliminating it helps transform your mind into a powerful concentrating apparatus.

Increased creativity: While you may believe that a messy studio, desk, or home office helps you work on your tasks work better, it is sensible to think that your creative juices will get going when you are in a clutter-free environment. Having your attention divided between lots of stimuli usually leads to higher stress levels and reduced productivity and creativity.

Eliminating emotional baggage: Having too much stuff is an emotional dilemma you can choose to ignore but will find very difficult to succeed in. You could end up spending days going through them and getting your emotions stirred by all those memories, both the good and the bad. The reality is that how clutter affects you typically does not have anything to do with how much clutter there is. For instance, a former best friend's painting that you hung over your bed can cause you to experience a more intense emotional turmoil than a closet filled with messed up extra towels and sheets. To put it simply, naming something as a form of clutter depends less on how it looks and more on how it makes you feel. If you find yourself feeling less satisfied or inspired in your home, take that as a cue to identifying the things that need to be disposed of. Save yourself from going through the emotional roller coaster and get rid of those items that only weigh you down emotionally.

Effortless money saving: If you think trying to save money is as enjoyable as getting punched in the stomach, you will be surprised to know that practicing the minimalist lifestyle allows you to save money like it is the most natural thing to do in the world. Without even trying, the money you would have spent on impulse buying ends up accumulating in the bank. Because minimalism and decluttering help you get your priorities straight, it becomes easier for you to pass up on buying the latest purse in favor of saving up for that grand vacation with your family. By resisting the relentless call of consumerism, you find yourself gaining additional funds you can use to pursue your dream of getting a new degree, taking up cooking classes, or traveling around the world. Minimalism and decluttering make you realize how sensible and more pleasurable it is to pass up on the feeling of gratification that purchasing the newest gadget brings so that you could funnel your funds on your hobbies instead.

Less stress: The more belongings you have, the more you feel stressed over having to look after them as well as getting them repaired when they get broken or lost. You may be all too familiar with that keys + phone + wallet routine that never fails to take place before you leave for work each morning, or that nonstop checking of your passport and boarding passes as you head through airport security. You may not have control over the necessities, but you do have the power to get rid of your extra possessions in order to eliminate the stress and anxiety that their background buzz brings.

Improved health: Spending less time at the hardware store attempting to outdo your next-door neighbor allows you to find the time to finally pursue your fitness goals. You probably used to constantly be telling yourself that you simply do not have the time to go to the gym, but living the minimalist way now enables you to practice yoga, take up running, or play with your kids at the park.

# Chapter 3 Signs and Symptoms of a Cluttered Life

Clutter has the tendency to creep the moment you relax your minimalism and decluttering efforts, which is why getting rid of all the clutter in your life should be an ongoing process. To stay on top of your mess-free game, make sure to heed the following signs of a decluttered life:

1. Difficulty in finding things
   Have you stopped to think about the amount of time you spend on a daily basis, just searching for your keys? Do you find it hard to look for the Sharpie at the exact moment you need to use it? Do you ever feel like crying as you wonder where you just placed your lip balm? Misplacing those everyday items on a regular basis or spending a big chunk of your time trying to find them is a sign that you need to practice minimalism and decluttering in your life. Having an organized home that is free from clutter helps you rest assured that all of your possessions have a place and that each of them is in its place. This means you have an idea about the exact location of each item since it requires no

effort to place it back to where it belongs. On the flip side, living with extra clutter at home is conducive to putting items down in the place where you were done using them instead of returning them to their specific places. Clutter simply prevents you noticing that certain things in your home are out of place.

2. Lack of clear space on flat surfaces
   The easiest way of making sure your home stays clutter-free is to keep all your flat surfaces clear. This truly makes sense, especially when you realize that flat surfaces somehow always manage to collect all sorts of clutter. Your flat surfaces are highly likely to get filled up when you possess too many belongings in your home. This is the reason you should avoid placing decorative fixtures, miscellaneous items, and other items not used on a daily basis on your tables, countertops, dresser tops, floors, and other flat surfaces.

3. Lack of empty floor space
   You may not realize it, but the easiest way to instantly make your home feel cluttered is to start messing up your floors. When you have too much stuff that you have to make use of your entire floor space to hold them, it is a distinct sign that you are living a cluttered life. Being in a situation where every inch of your floors is home to

some storage item or furniture makes you even more prone to creating more clutter because you will have to find the extra time and effort to clean everything. The way everything feels too crowded in your home, one out-of-place thing is all it takes to make your entire home appear messy.

4. Overflowing laundry basket
It is a clear signal that your life needs minimalism and decluttering when the laundry baskets start overflowing. This is because having more clothes translates to more laundry to tackle. Keeping up with all the washing, rinsing, drying, and folding of your clothes takes up too much of your time. To avoid the prospect of piled up laundry all the time, simply choose to own fewer clothes.

5. Difficulty in closing cabinets and drawers
You may find yourself needing to forcefully shove your clothes down into drawers just so you could close the latter. Your cabinets in the kitchen may also be difficult to shut unless you make sure the handles on the pots and pans inside were turned just so. You may find it requires all your might to simply get your hall closets and bathroom cabinet closed. All of these are clear indicators of a clutter problem in your life.

6. More dishes than you can handle
   If you had to choose between washing out a plate and reaching for a clean one in the cupboard, you most probably would go for the latter. The problem is that this is exactly what leads to your dishes piling up in the sink.

7. Trouble with fitting the car in the garage
   Although it is alright to store stuff in the garage, you know you have a problem with clutter in your life when you can no longer park your car in it.

8. Unhealthy eating patterns
   A Psychological Science study has shown that individuals who live in orderly surroundings tend to eat healthier snacks than people who live in cluttered homes. Because clutter can be stressful for your brain, you end up being more prone to going for comfort foods or resorting to overeating as a way of coping with the stress.

9. Increased stress
   A study on social psychology and personality has indicated that individuals with cluttered homes, especially those with plenty of unfinished projects, had higher incidences of fatigue, depression, and raised cortisol (stress hormone) levels than people who expressed having "restorative" and "restful" living

environments. The same study indicated that when cortisol levels do not decrease at a normal rate within the day, a person ends up being more likely to suffer from chronic stress, worsen his disease symptoms, and increase his mortality risk.

10. Triggered respiratory problems
A study on healthy homes has revealed that cluttered homes tend to have more dust that could either trigger or worsen breathing issues. The more stuff you have piling up in your home, the more dust is actually generated, which then creates the perfect living environments for dust mites and other pests. Respiratory problems become more serious when you find it harder to reach and clean your home's different areas.

11. Threatened safety
A study on mental health has given out a warning on having too much clutter in your home, suggesting that serious fire hazards can be created when paper, cardboard boxes, and clothes are blocking your windows and doorways.

12. Isolation from others
How clean or cluttered your home is can actually have an effect on whether or not you will want to invite people to come over. A study by Rubbermaid found that fifty percent of the people they surveyed

said they would rather not have friends comes over to visit if their homes are cluttered.

13. Wrecked relationships
Individuals who are prone to hoarding constantly find it hard to part with their belongings because they believe they need to save those things. They can also feel distress over the mere thought of disposing of their possessions. Such a situation can cause a marriage to suffer. The cluttered person's spouse is always bothered by their living environment and ends up expressing his or her discomfort by judging, name-calling, making negative comments, being irritable, and being angry.

14. Not so happy kids
Your kids bear the negative impact of living in a cluttered home as well. A study on mental health found that children living in extremely cluttered homes usually feel more distressed, are less happy, and find it difficult to make friends.

15. Drained finances
If you have bad spending habits, know that these can also be encouraged by the constant presence of clutter in your home. Living in a messy home makes it too easy for you to misplace stuff, and when you

fail to find a child's favorite toy, the yoga mat, or something else you need, your tendency is to go out and purchase another one. You can easily find yourself getting into debt when you combine this habit with spending too much money in hoarding stuff. Having a cluttered home also makes it hard for you to find your bank statements, credit card bills, and other financial documents. Losing track of another bill leads to making yet another late payment. All of a sudden, you find yourself having to deal with higher interest rates, extra fees, and collection agents.

16. Derailed career
    A cluttered lifestyle can hinder you from getting promoted at work. Your job performance can be severely affected by an unorganized briefcase, a messy desk, and a lack of defined filing system. A study on career building revealed that twenty-eight percent of employers are hesitant to give someone a promotion if he has a cluttered work space. Clutter also makes you more likely to miss work. A research on mental health determined that there is a link between compulsive hoarding and an average of 7 missed work days each month, which is more than the number of work days missed by individuals suffering from other disorders

related to mood, anxiety, and substance use.

17. Reduced productivity
Living in cluttered surroundings hinders your ability to concentrate. A study on neuroscience has shown that seeing different stimuli all at once can cause you to lose focus, as those stimuli are competing for your brain's attention. This means your productivity is decreased when you are looking at a desk cluttered with pens, papers, photos, and snacks. The study also revealed that having a clutter-free work surrounding promotes productivity, reduces moodiness, and increases the ability to process information.

# Chapter 4 A Minimalist Guide to Immediately Decluttering Your Life

Like many individuals, you are probably holding onto stuff that are either of questionable quality or are partially broken, believing that you need to have them around in order to get your money's worth or to have a back-up. But this mindset only leads to purchasing more things than you dispose of, which results in multiples of the same item and a collection of spare pieces that you know are useless. The good news is that minimalism and decluttering can help you combat this attitude, and the tips below will specifically enable you to achieve that.

1. Set defined goals
   The fact that you desire to live a minimalist and decluttered life means that you are presently in a situation where you seek order and peace of mind. You are probably persistently stressing over a continually decreasing bank balance, or are at your wits' end trying to relax in a living room that resembles an ancient homestead. For you to reach the point

where you experience a sense of accomplishment and notice a positive change, it is important that you figure out the problem that needs to be solved so that you can identify the steps you should take. You may feel as though you are not making any progress if you do not have some barometer for success, which is why it is necessary to define your goals, put them into writing, and constantly reflect on them. This will help you stay motivated as well as avoid thinking that you are just wasting your time.

2. Begin with baby steps
Setting a goal is not worth anything if it is something that is unattainable. Even if you truly want to, living a minimalist and decluttered life does not mean you will be turning from a satisfied consumer clearing out shelves of top-quality crystal ware into a nomad living out of a backpack. The degree of minimalism and decluttering you want to achieve is not your priority here. You should start small first and take steps to identify your progress in order to slowly but surely reach your goals. It helps to select a single category to explore at first, such as a decluttered kitchen or a minimalist work space. Doing so will allow you to figure out a strategy that will suit you as well as to avoid experiencing setbacks that can prevent you from keeping on.

3. Go for quality
   This is something you have probably heard over and over again, but it is true that quality trumps quantity. Rather than purchasing too much stuff that are cheap and made with flimsy materials, choose to buy a few quality items that you know will be put to good use for a long time.
   Another thing that is great about going for quality instead of quantity is that you will be helping reduce waste and preserve our environment. It would be wise to consider investing in products that are manufactured through ethical means, can be used for multiple purposes, and do not require you to replace them that often.

4. Nix any duplicates
   One of the easiest ways you could do to begin decluttering your home and living a minimalist lifestyle is to gather all duplicate items that are merely collecting dust on your tables and shelves, which are already burdened with the weight of all those numerous trinkets you chose to keep just because. Put them all in a box and store in a place where you will not be able to see them for a short while. If after the allotted time has passed, you feel that you never really missed the items, such that you do not even have the faintest idea why you had them at all, then you could

go ahead and give them up for donation or simply throw them away.

5. Set yourself little challenges
Count yourself blessed if you are one who can get the job done under pressure and who is always up for a challenge. Living a minimalist and decluttered lifestyle is something that will surely satisfy your competitive nature. Consider giving yourself small challenges to overcome in your quest to practice minimalism and decluttering. This is an effective strategy for keeping yourself from getting bored, keeping track of your progress, and making sure you stay focused and motivated. If you are not sure about where you should begin, you can challenge yourself to pare your wardrobe down to 25 pieces, to use only such-and-such amount when you go grocery shopping, to give away a small number of your belongings to charity each month, or to carry just a backpack on your next vacation trip. You might even encourage your family and friends to join you in your project to really motivate you into accomplishing your minimalism and decluttering goals.

6. Try the Minimalist Game
The Minimalist Game is a minimalist and decluttering strategy that makes a game out of the experience, one that involves

posting on social media the #minsgame hashtag each month.

- It basically encourages you to make sure that the number of items you declutter per day corresponds to what day of the month it is. This means you would be decluttering one thing on the 1st day of the month, two things on the 2nd day, three things on the 3rd day, and so on.

- By the time you reach the end of the month, you should have been able to get rid of 496 things from your house. It is important that you make sure to follow this challenge through, and it works most effectively if you have friends and family members join you in a friendly competition.

- The advantage to following the Minimalist Game is that you will have gotten rid of a ton of decluttered items at the end of a month. Having removed about five hundred things from your life is a big accomplishment, and it is up to you how many months you want in a row to play this game. It is a great way of developing in yourself the confidence to make decisions and to be able to let go of your possessions.

- One disadvantage to this minimalism and decluttering strategy, however, is the fact that you need to be consistent on a daily basis. Failing to do so would make it easy for you to get off track. Because it is essentially a game, this method increases in difficulty with each level, which makes it harder to keep up with if you are not consistent with it. You also have to go to extra lengths to search for items to declutter and discard towards the month's end. You would not want to have just twenty items to show for a long day's work.

7. Give the KonMari Method a go
Author Marie Kondo popularized this method of decluttering the home, and it has become more well-known due to the fact that she has sold more than 4 million copies of her book on the subject.

- At the heart of this decluttering method is the premise that you select the items you want to hold onto and then get rid of the rest, rather than deciding beforehand which items should be disposed of.

You will get started on the KonMari method by collecting each and every item you possess in a certain category, and then place them in one big pile. For instance, gather all of the T-shirts you own and place them on the floor. Run your fingers through each garment to help you truly recognize the feeling it evokes from you, and then you should ask yourself whether or not the T-shirt sparks joy in your heart.

- A great advantage to following the KonMari method is that, being especially thorough, you give yourself the chance to compare all items belonging to a category. This way, you can eliminate any duplicate items as well as compare your not-so-liked pieces to the ones that are of better quality. The KonMari method effectively helps you make progress in decluttering in particular categories in different parts of your home all at once.

- The downside to this method is the fact that in requires a big chunk of your time. It also involves having to sort through your entire home in order to declutter stuff. Rather than concentrating on a single room, you will need to pull things out of the house all at the same time, resulting in the possibility that you may have to totally uproot your house.

8. Take a shot at the Four Box Method
The Four Box decluttering method is one that gives you the flexibility to handle all of the things that are creating a mess in your home, for the length of time and how often you find it is convenient for you to do so. Because you will be sorting your belongings into 4 categories, you will be able to decide what to do to each item that is out of place.

- Basically, you will be setting up 4 boxes in the room you will be working on, and attach a corresponding label to each: Put Away, Throw Away, Give Away, and Undecided. You pick up the items causing clutter in the room and put them in one of those 4 boxes, then process every box, keeping the label on it in mind. What is great about this method is that gives you the flexibility to use the Undecided box in case you cannot figure out just yet what you should be doing to a certain item.

- This method gives you the advantage of decluttering your

home in a straightforward manner, especially when there is a specific category for every item. It prevents you from getting stuck with a certain item because you can reconsider the items you place in the Undecided category at a later date. The Four Box method simply allows you to practice minimalism and decluttering at the pace that you are comfortable with.

- The downside to the Four Box method is the fact that your Undecided box can turn into a problem when it eventually gets loaded with too many items. This is especially true in those situations where you are just too tired from all the decluttering you have been doing so that you find it convenient to simply toss this and that item in the Undecided category. This is why it would be wise to hold off having to use the Undecided box if you can help it.

9. Have a Packing Party
   The Packing Party method is one that will take the minimalism and decluttering endeavor to extreme levels. This is a particularly effective strategy to use if you have definite plans of moving to another house. Although it does require you to put

in lots of work and preparation, going through the method ensures that you will succeed in your decluttering mission.

- The Packing Party method involves inviting your friends over to your house and getting them to help you pack all of your belongings into boxes, with the understanding that it will be as if you are moving to a new house.
You will only be able to take out those things you actually use over the next several months, and you should make the decision to either donate or sell those items left sitting inside their boxes once three months have passed.

- The upside to this method is that it will truly allow you to let go of those things that you never really use. It helps you realize that you never really think of those items that you never see, so there is a big chance that you would not even miss those that are placed in the boxes. The Packing Party method is an effective decluttering method to follow when it is time for you to actually move to somewhere new. In your new house, you simply get the things you have to use out of their boxes, rather than immediately unpacking all boxes.

- Following this method would not be sensible if you are not actually moving to a new house. It requires a tremendous amount of effort and time to haul out your belongings and put them into boxes. You also have to take into account the money you have to spend on buying all those boxes. The Packing Party method is also not worth the effort for seasonal stuff and other items that you do not really use on a regular basis.

10. Give the One Method a try

The One Method decluttering strategy is a mixed bag of other similar methods. It involves getting rid of something each day for a certain period of time. That something may be a single item, a single box filled with different items, or a single filled bag each day.

- This method effectively helps instill in yourself a habit of removing clutter from your life on a regular basis. Because you are taking clutter out of the house each day, it becomes easier for you to make decluttering a part of your lifestyle.

- The One Method allows you to be in control of what system to use in decluttering your home. You can determine the number of items you would prefer to get rid of each day based as you see fit.

- This method, however, can be hard to do consistently, especially if your schedule is packed or if you are going away to travel. If you are more interested in decluttering in one big purge instead of doing it one day at a time, then the One Method may not work for you.

# Chapter 5 Creating a Minimalist and Decluttered Home

Applying minimalism and decluttering to your home will help you reclaim your space by letting go of everyday junk as well as excess décor and furniture. You will achieve an aesthetic that boasts of clean and simple surfaces, walls that are not covered with busy artwork and prints, and bookshelves and closets that are not drowning in all kinds of knickknacks.

When you live in a minimalist and decluttered home, you will realize how peaceful it feels not to have that many belongings around. You savor the feeling of being stress-free as a result of being clutter-free. You discover the contentment that comes with no longer feeling the need to buy as much as you used to. You can rest assured knowing that the things you truly need are met at home, so that you do not have to buy more in order to fill something lacking in your life.

To create a minimalist and decluttered home, your goal is to pare everything down to the basics. This could mean your bedroom will be rid of miscellaneous papers, numerous trinkets, and piles of clothing and will only have a bed and a nightstand that can adequately provide your need for comfort and warmth. Regardless of which room it is you want to transform into an organized and streamlined space, you have to make sure that it meets the following conditions:

- All your stuff are neatly arranged: A clutter-free look is what makes your space or home so appealing to look at and to be in.
- Any unnecessary furniture is absent: You are going for simplicity in creating your minimalist, decluttered room, which is why placing certain furniture pieces in it just because you want other people to know that you own them is out of the question.
- Quality rules the day: Your home is filled with quality pieces that you have carefully picked out, instead of being stuffed with cheap items that only add clutter to any space.

Remember those three conditions and it should be easy for you to follow the tips and tricks below on how to turn every room in your house into the clutter-free, minimalist space you have always wanted.

## LIVING ROOM

<u>Declutter your living room by:</u>

1. Sorting all items into the Keep, Store, Donate, or Dispose category
   After going through the items you have decluttered, make the decision about whether an item should be kept in your living room, stored in another part of the house, thrown out for good, or donated to someone who find some use for it. You need to be clear about the stuff that are no longer a necessity in your life, even if it means having to chuck your late grandmother's prized hefty furniture.

   - Spring cleaning is an ideal time to go through your belongings and figure out which stays and which goes. Accumulating lots of things is a natural part of life, although you could always do away with the trouble of living a cluttered house that is too crowded for comfort and is difficult to clean.

   - Consider earning some money from your decluttered possessions by selling them at a garage sale or through the Internet.

2. Disposing of any broken items
Be firm about throwing out any item that is broken or is just no longer functional. If you prefer not to hold on to some items that are still serviceable, you can always give them away to friends or donate them to charities.

3. Look below the sofa cushions and remove all the coins and other bits and pieces you may find.

4. On a daily basis, remove any old newspapers and magazines from the living room and place those you want to keep in a magazine rack or a drawer.

5. Make it a habit to pull out any item that does not belong in your living room, then transfer to another part of the house.

6. Make use of storage solutions

- *Cubby holes*: You can place your kids' toys in wicker boxes or plastic bins, which can then be stored in cubby hole units.

- *Bins and boxes*: Give your video game consoles and television remotes a designated place by storing them in bins and boxes when they are not used.

- *Baskets and trunks*: A leather trunk is an elegant place to store things and can even be used as foot stool or a side table. Meanwhile, newspapers and magazines can be kept inside a leather basket to prevent them from looking cluttered.

- *Shelving*: Shelving units allow you to get your belongings off the floor to help give the impression that you have a large living room space.

- *Built-in storage*: Ottoman foot stools and coffee tables that come with drawers enable you to own furniture that also function as storage units.

- *Mirrors*: You can use mirrors to add to the size of your living room with the way they create a less cluttered appearance and an illusion of space. Keep in mind that using a larger mirror results in a larger illusion of space. Consider placing a mirror opposite the view you would prefer to be reflected. If you place a mirror opposed to a window, you will be adding greenery and natural light into a rather small space.

<u>Give your living room a minimalist style by:</u>

1. Thinking about scale
   This is an important thing to consider if you want your living room to achieve the minimalist and decluttered look. You would never dream of just cramming your living room with too many small furniture pieces, as this will only result in making your space feel too cramped. What you can do instead is to mix things up – add a few larger furniture pieces to coordinate with your existing smaller ones. For instance, you can invest in a couch that is L-shaped to give the living room a nicely filled-out look as well as provide adequate space for other furniture pieces to fill in. Just keep in mind your living room's scale in figuring out the items you will add to it to give it a more open vibe.

2. Bring in the green
   A few well-placed plants in your living room will give it a clean and fresh feel

that adds to the minimalist look. Consider distributing two to three houseplants in vibrant green colors around the space. Place them in neutral colored planters or elegant glass jars to add to the decluttered feel. Go for houseplants that will thrive in the amount of sunlight that enters your living room.

3. Go for floating shelves
   Compared to those clunky shelving units, floating shelves do a better job in making your space feel more decluttered. Their modern design makes them great for housing one to two plants, a handful of trinkets, and books. Install one in your living room to automatically lend it a cleaner, more contemporary, and brighter look.

4. Choose the right colors
   There is a good reason the all-white option is a favorite among many people. A living room with bare white walls, a white rug, and a beige couch give off an airier and a brighter vibe that is perfect for those wanting to have a minimalist style living room.

   - If you would rather not use the all-white palette in your space, you could try bringing in design elements in neutral tones to complement your few pieces of white furniture.

- If your living room is already awash in neutral colors, try giving it pops of bright colors by adding in wall accents, a woven rug, or your favorite artwork. It also helps to make use of various textures and tones in your same-color furniture, rug, and walls.

- Another great idea would be to use some sort of color coding in your bookshelves. You can instantly add style to the living room by simply organizing those books based on color. Just keep in mind that it is important to coordinate your colors and to ensure that everything is in sync with your chosen overall color palette. Otherwise, your living room will end up looking and feeling junky from all that contrasting colors and textures.

5. Keep stored items out of the way
You probably have piles of random items like bills and magazines stacked on different areas in the living room. To achieve the minimalist and uncluttered look you are going for, make sure to store those items in a storage bin or a

pretty basket and bring somewhere out of sight.

6. Make sure items are paired well together
Aside from making your living room look clutter-free, choosing a unified color and design scheme will help you truly channel the minimalist style. The easiest way to do this is to see to it that all items in the living room can be paired well without a hitch. An example would be making sure that everything, from the tiniest jar to the sofa, have a classic and simple design and come in colors that allow them to be at home with the space's colors.

## **KITCHEN**

<u>Declutter your kitchen by:</u>

1. Clearing out the following items

   - Dish towels: Evaluate your dish towels and get rid of the ones that have seen better days. Take a close look at the ones that remain and determine if you truly need to use all of them. If this is not the case, you could donate them to others who could still use them. If they are no longer in good enough condition, you can repurpose them into rags. Your larger dish towels will be most welcomed by animal shelters.

- Kitchen gadgets: It might seem so modern and cool to own kitchen gadgets, but if you are going to be honest about it, do you really use them that often? Rather than waste precious space by letting them sit pretty in your kitchen, consider donating those that are no longer used. The same goes for those with functions that could easily be done by another existing item in the kitchen. Never try to save something to have a backup and decide to keep only those items you actually use.

- Small kitchen appliances: If the tasks that are supposed to be done by your smaller kitchen appliances could easily be done by another, then make the decision to sell or donate the former. This way, you get to remove clutter, earn a bit of money, and reclaim precious space.

- Baking ware: Get rid of those extra cookie sheets, old muffin tins, and unused pie pans.

- Cleaning supplies: Evaluate your cleaning supplies, then get rid of the ones that are not used anymore. Mix the contents of multiple bottles if they contain the same product to save on space. Make sure to place the almost-empty bottles toward your stash's front part so that they are the first to get used up.

- Spices: You may have a handful of spices still hanging around inside your cupboards without ever being used. Toss those that you never use anymore or if the flavors are no longer there. You can then simply stock your cupboard with basic spices that you actually use. If, down the line, you have to have a specific spice for a specific recipe, you could easily just buy it in a small bulk.

- Pantry items: Let go of those items that are already expired, as well as the ones that are already opened and will not be used anytime soon.

- Fridge/freezer: Give those items in the fridge that are past their expiration dates a quick toss. Do the same to items in your fridge that appear to be freezer-burned. And remember to check all the bottles' expiration dates to avoid accidentally using something that has already gone from bad to gross.

- Food keepers: Make sure to match all lids with the right bottoms. Get rid of anything that has no match, then donate all that remaining ones that are no longer useful or needed.

- Countertops: A cluttered countertop could easily make your entire kitchen look messy. All that mess also makes your countertop even harder to keep clean, even after a good wipe down. Dispose of papers that you do not really need, decorative kitchen accessories that have lost their appeal, and small appliances that you do not actually use regularly.

- Coffee mugs and glasses: Make sure that the current set of glasses and mugs you have in the kitchen are ones that you truly need and use. Make sure to recycle the ones that are broken or chipped. Throw out any mismatched pieces, keep a few pieces from your collection of coffee mugs, and donate everything else.

- Junk drawer: Like most people, you may have that junk drawer in the kitchen, filled with all sorts of items, most of which are not what you actually use or need. Give up anything that fits into either categories, such as old candles and batteries, extra tools, cords, and phone chargers, and excess office supplies.

- Cookbooks: Go through all your cookbooks and pick out those you have not used anymore so you could donate them. You can just copy the contents of those cookbooks that contain only a few recipes, store the handwritten notes in a recipe box, and dispose of the cookbooks. If there are recipes you would like to follow in recipe magazines, you can simply tear them out and then keep them in a special binder.

- Medicine and vitamins: You can store these items in the kitchen, as long as it will be in a cooler area where the stove's or other appliances' steam could not reach them. It also helps to make sure all medicines and vitamins are updated and are safely out of reach of little kids' hands.

2. Ditching the extra knives
   You do not need 18 knives sitting there in your kitchen in order for you to properly prepare a decent dinner. You most likely need just 3, and can do away with the knife collection you bought with your first salary, the beautiful knife set given to you as a wedding gift, and the 10 bread knives you have ended up buying after all these years. Instead of relying on too many knives, invest in just three pieces that you will actually use on a regular basis. Buy yourself a high-quality bread knife, paring knife, and chef's knife and ditch the existing knife set you currently own but never use.

3. Giving up your microwave
   It might be hard to imagine getting by without your microwave, but it can be done. Whatever it is you can prepare in the microwave can certainly be prepared in the oven or on the stovetop as well, and it would actually taste better. The advantage to using the microwave is the speed at which it can heat your meals, but that affects the food's quality and flavor. The truth is that letting go of your microwave will spur you into cooking more whole foods and relying less on heavily processed packaged foods.

4. Cutting back on the dishware
   This does not mean you should get rid of your treasured china. It simply means keeping only those dishes you actually use and letting go of the remaining 20 or so plates as well as the 5 types of wine glasses using up valuable space in your cabinets.

5. Making do with just enough cookware
   If you are secretly envious of your neighbors' fully equipped kitchen, stop. You should know that they are not actually using all of that stuff. All it really takes for anyone to be able to cook is one chopping board (you do not have to bend over backwards it in different shapes and sizes), one to two sauce pots and frying pans, one stock pot, one cast iron pan, and a Dutch oven. You can have a blast cooking up a storm in your kitchen with these items alone, so donate or throw out the rest of your clunky pans and pots.

6. Letting go of extra gadgets
   It is important to recognize the difference between kitchen gadgets that are essential for food preparation and those that you could easily do without. You can definitely use that vegetable peeler, but any simple knife can easily replace that garlic press egg separator,

and an avocado slicer, and you will have no use of a KitchenAid mixer if you do not even bake. Go for quality, not novelty, when it comes to choosing your kitchen gadgets.

7. Getting creative with storage
   If you are going to go minimalist with your kitchen, make sure you have a proper storage system. You do not have to buy anything fancy or expensive. Some ideas to try include:

   - Getting hold of a cooking caddy: Store your spices and condiments in a rack that you could easily carry with you. Although you may want to have your favorite spices, salt, and cooking oils right beside the stove, especially when you do use them on a daily basis, you would not want them to clutter up the counter space all the time. Consider keeping them organized in a cooking caddy that you can just hide away in a cabinet once you are done preparing a meal.

   - Securing those dish towels: Although it makes sense to hang your kitchen towels from the dishwasher or oven door (it makes for a convenient spot to dry towels), what happens is that they always manage to slip off. To prevent this from ever happening again, try folding the towel in the form you prefer, then attach a Velcro strip on the front as well as on the back. You could either stitch the Velcro in place or opt for those fabric ones that you could just iron over. Once done, slip the dish towel through the dishwasher or oven's door handle and simply have the Velcro ends meet.

- Rolling out the kitchen cabinet: Save yourself from the agony of having no space left in your kitchen cabinets to store anything by installing kitchen cabinet rollouts. They provide extra storage room to your cabinets while making it easy for you to locate any item.

- Storing food in a basket: One of the worst things that could happen to you when you get home after a trip to the grocery store would have to be finding out that you have no counter or fridge space left to unload the fresh fruits and vegetables you just bought. Solve this issue by hanging a wire basket (single or tiered) from the kitchen ceiling. Aside from providing visual appeal to the kitchen space, it also serves as a catchall container for your oranges, apples, bananas, potatoes, garlic, and onions.

- Reaching for a spice rack: The spice rack is your best friend when it comes to having a place to store our small jars of cinnamon, thyme, and oregano. Although you could always store your spices in the cupboard, it can be too easy to mess them up as you hurriedly rummage through them while you are cooking. Get yourself a spice rack and fill it with your labeled spice jars.

<u>Give your kitchen a minimalist style by:</u>

1. Keeping all kitchen items organized
Organizing your kitchen ware, table ware, and utensils will help in making your kitchen space look clutter-free and in creating a minimalist feel. Make sure to assign every kitchen item to its own designated closed compartment, if possible, to avoid any clutter from being seen.

2. Making sure all parts of the kitchen is clean and clear

Never leave any leftover food around and always remember to wipe all surfaces. It also helps to see to it that no dirty dishes are left stacked up in the sink. Clean everything on a regular basis and make sure the kitchen furniture pieces are always in order.

3. Placing kitchen items in streamlined containers
   It is easy to find minimalist-style jars to contain your salt, sugar, flour, and other cooking items. Streamlined containers allow you to minimize or eliminate your kitchen's usually cluttered look. Go for transparent or simple white jars for a strongly minimalist vibe.

4. Sticking to one color scheme
   Pick out a color scheme for your kitchen furniture, cabinets, and walls to make sure that you achieve a cohesive look that whispers minimalist. Focus on using just two to three colors.

5. Using kitchen items in the same color
   If possible, pick the same color kitchen items that complement the theme you have chosen for your kitchen space. For instance, you could choose a white food processor if your kitchenware is mostly white. Doing so helps in creating an elegant and harmonious look and feel that is so minimalist.

6. Going for appliances with a streamlined design
   How your refrigerator, toaster, kitchen appliances, and other kitchen appliances are shaped and designed has a significant impact on how your entire kitchen space will look and feel. This is why you should steer clear any single item, like an ugly-looking toaster, or risk ruining the whole vibe of your minimalist kitchen.

7. Getting simplistic kitchenware or utensils
   Your kitchen's minimalist appeal can also be enhanced by utensils and kitchenware that have beautiful designs. Go for gray, black, bare metal, or other basic colors instead of experimenting with bright yellow, deep red, and other loud colors that go against what the minimalist aesthetic is supposed to be.

8. Using simple lighting
   Consider investing in modern-design lighting fixtures for your kitchen that do a good job of lighting the entire space. Instead of table lamps, go for wall lights or hanging lights that are better at making your kitchen appear well-lit and interesting. It is also important to make sure that the bulbs' color temperature suits the minimalist look you are going

for. If you want a homey, cozy feel, then warm lighting may be your best bet.

## **BEDROOM**

<u>Declutter your bedroom by:</u>

1. Taking out unnecessary furniture
   One way of making your bedroom appear mess-free and minimalist in style is to get rid of any furniture that do not really serve a purpose besides taking up too much space. Doing this helps free up floor space that can make your bedroom feel and look way bigger than it is.

2. Sorting stuff into 3 piles
   Doing so allows you to easily figure out which items are worth keeping, worth storing, and should be thrown out. Place your worth keeping stuff in a plastic bin or a drawer. Items that are to be stored should be placed in labeled containers before putting away in your chosen storage area. Sort through the items you want to throw out an decide on which can be sold, donated, or dispatched to a junk collector.

3. Giving attention to your clothes
   Go through all your articles of clothing and clear out anything you no longer

wear or simply do not fit you anymore. You can then throw them out or give them away to charity.

4. Taking care of your bedside table

- Choose to have just a handful of necessary items on your bedside table, such as an alarm, a book, a water bottle, and a bedside lamp.

- Avoid placing your cellphone on the bedside table. Make sure to place it far from the bed during the night. This will help keep you from giving in to using it for calling and texting, sending emails, posting on social media, and as an alarm clock.

- If you feel that you must have a few decorative items, such as a candle or a photo frame, on the bedside table, go for those that are color-coordinated to make sure everything looks clutter-free.

- In case you have other belongings that should be kept in your bedside table, go for a bigger one that comes with cupboards or shelves. The key is to make sure everything is organized, which is why it makes sense to place small storage boxes inside the unit.

5. Getting your clothes organized
Having organized clothes will help you quickly get to work each morning as well as ensure that your bedside table has the minimalist and decluttered style that you want to achieve. When putting fresh laundry away, make sure to put same items together; for instance, skirts with skirts and long-sleeved shirts with other long-sleeved tops. Soon, you will have a streamlined wardrobe that will help make dressing up in the morning something to look forward to.

6. Get out-of-season garments out of the way
Out-of-season clothing and accessories are best placed under the bed or atop your wardrobe. It would not be sensible to have them in circulation during the months when you are not going to use them at all.

7. Throw out certain footwear
Do not hesitate to donate or dispose of your shoes that no longer fit or have not been worn for a long time.

8. Ditch some of your accessories
Pamper yourself by using bed furnishings and linen that feel

comfortable and luxurious, but see to it that your bed remains easy to make. You will only end with a disheveled bed if you have too many throws and cushions on it.

9. Say no to broken items
   This goes for ornaments, books, and other items in the bedroom that you need to get rid of because they are broken. If they are still in good condition, consider donating them.

10. Put clothes away as a habit
    Make sure to always put your clothes away at night. It would also be wise to consistently lay out the clothes you plan on wearing the next day. Doing so will create a positive impact on your day as well as help prevent you from creating clutter while getting dressed.

11. Using clever storage solutions
    Your bedroom is your designated place for relaxation in the home, so remember to factor in storage space in redesigning it. it would be difficult for you to relax if you are constantly tripping on clutter as you walk around the bedroom. To maintain your space's minimalist and decluttered feel, heed the following bedroom storage tips:

- Sliding wardrobe doors: An effective strategy for maximizing bedroom space is to have sliding wardrobe doors installed. You can get them customized to accommodate your belongings as well as coordinate with your existing interiors.

- Under-bed storage containers: Make use of the space under your bed, where you can keep storage boxes or bags that hold items you seldom use, like your blankets and out-of-season garments.

- A bedside table with drawers: If yours already comes with built-in drawers, make sure to avoid overfilling them with items that can inevitably turn into clutter. Knowing that you have clutter hidden in those drawers can still negatively affect your desire to live a minimalist lifestyle.

- Ottoman bed: A bedroom where every item has its own place is one of the most effective ways you can practice minimalism and live without clutter. By having an ottoman bed inside the bedroom, you will have yourself a built-in decluttering and storage system. Just remember to take into consideration the size that fits your minimalist needs.

- Hidden storage system: Consider investing in high-quality storage solutions to replace those chunky and unattractive plastic containers you have sitting inside your bedroom. This way, you can rest assured that each of your belongings has its own designated place, and you can keep yourself from buying more items to add to your collection.

- Shelving: This type of bedroom storage solution will allow you to keep your belongings off the floor as well as create the impression of a bigger bedroom.

- Stackable shelves: Instead of trying to make do with an existing wardrobe space that seems conducive to clutter, try adding stackable shelves or installing additional rods to work with the hanging shelf and bar that are already built in.

- Bins, baskets, and boxes: Make use of bins, baskets, and boxes in case you must have additional storage units in your bedroom. You can then either display them or store them out of the way.

Give your bedroom a minimalist style by:

1. Letting in natural light
   A minimalist bedroom's most notable feature is its lighting, which is emphasized by having just few furniture pieces in the space. You could either pull back the curtains or use sheer ones to bring natural light in, which can help the bedroom achieve a minimalist and more open ambience.

2. Using bedding in neutral colors
   Creamy white, pale gray, and soft beige are some examples of neutral tones that you can use in creating your minimalist bedroom. They will radiate a Zen-like feel in your room, in contrast with using crazy patterns in clashing colors. Going for a neutral palette also allows you to play with your accent colors.

3. Going for neutral-colored accessories
   This does not mean you have to go out on a buying spree for ten throw pillows in khaki tone. It just means sticking to your chosen neutral scheme when buying a new accessory for the bedroom. Retain your space's minimalist vibe by steering away from color clashes.

4. Sticking to a single piece of artwork
   Going for a minimalist aesthetic for your bedroom does not imply covering the walls' entire surface with paintings and photos, with the belief that these are what will complete your bedroom's look. In case you already have an existing small collection of artwork, you can pick that one piece that you love looking at the most. Hang it on the wall... and that is it. Adorning the walls with more accents will ruin the whole minimalist and decluttered aesthetic you are going for.

5. Picking just one shelf
   You may be able to keep your sentimental trinkets and other keepsakes, as long as you make sure they get stored in a single shelf.

6. Bringing in a plant
   Your minimalist and decluttered bedroom deserves a touch of earthiness that a well-chosen house plant can deliver. Plants let you perk up an otherwise bland, neutralized space, as long as it does not compete with your selected artwork and other accessories. Consider bringing a rubber plant into your bedroom. Other possible choices include fiddle leaf figs, a philodendron, and freshly-picked flowers.

7. Going for a simple bed frame
All bedrooms have a common denominator – they all have the bed as the entire space's foal point. This is why it is important that you choose the right bed frame, as it sets the tone for your bedroom's atmosphere. Your minimalist options include a platform bed, a metal bed frame, or a box spring.

8. Choosing a streamlined bed
Get your minimalist streak going by opting to furnish your bedroom with a platform bed in a sleek design instead of a four-poster bed, a carved sleigh bed, or a canopy bed. A minimalist bedroom's hallmark feature is the simple platform bed frame that is covered in plain neutral-colored bedding. Having that platform bed in your bedroom space allows you to do away with getting that rather bulky box spring. A platform bed is also minimalist in the sense that you only need to dress it up with a few toss pillows in a textured fabric to keep it looking proportioned and balanced.

9. Not forgetting to include small touches
You still have room to play around with certain artwork and patterns in decorating your minimalist bedroom. The only thing you will have to remember is you should keep the

elements in control. Make sure to pick out artwork and patterns that have restrained lines and that come with a limited palette. Stay away from small busy prints, large floral prints, complicated designs, and extravagant styles. What you want in your small touches are those that are not screaming for attention. The key is to anchor your minimalist bedroom on solid blocks of neutrals in order to create a sense of tranquility in the space. When it comes to artwork, you can hang just one big, well-selected piece that immediately calls you to feel calm and serene the moment you see it.

10. Minding your balance and symmetry
Harmony is one of minimalism's key elements, which is why it is important that you concentrate on your bedroom's size and scale. Filling a tiny bedroom with large furniture causes it to feel cramped, while bringing in small furniture pieces into an otherwise gigantic space results in a bedroom that just look off. Consider organizing your bedroom furniture and décor in such a way that the whole space looks orderly and neat. Making sure your bedroom looks proportioned and balanced helps move the eye smoothly throughout the space as well as give it a calm and controlled vibe.

# HOME OFFICE

<u>Declutter your home office and give it the minimalist treatment by:</u>

1. Working with one inbox
   If your work involves using paper – and lots of it – make sure to have an inbox parked on your desk. All of your documents, sticky notes, and phone messages should land on this tray. Never leave any paper littering your desk. Set aside a folder labeled as a "Working File" to hold the papers you are working on at the moment, then put away in a drawer. Remember to clear out the inbox tray on a daily basis; once you are done processing a paper, avoid putting it back. Your inbox should not serve as a paper storage bin.

2. Evaluating your paper priorities
   This will help you cut back on your constant yet unnecessary use of paper. You may find that you can simply keep certain files on your computer so that you never have to print them out. You might also stop keeping around paper copies of all the files you already have stored on the computer. Consider asking people to send memos and other work documents through email instead of faxing them to you. It also helps to take steps to avoid circulating documents by

using paper, such as signing up for online billing and unsubscribing to newsletters and catalogs that get sent to you by snail mail.

3. Opting to digitize your existing paperwork
   Consider investing in a scanner, an office equipment that does not take up as much space as all those papers it will be replacing. For documents that does not need to have a physical copy, it would be smart to convert them into bytes and bits, which means you will not have to deal with clutter and still get to keep the information.

4. Letting go of your landline phone and answering machine
   You can conduct business with the aid of your mobile phone as well as voice mail.

5. Taming your supplies
   Trim down your excessive collection office supplies if you will never really use them all. Donate the excess of your 200 folders, 500 paper clips, and 100 pens to family and friends. Next time, buy only what you need to use at the moment rather than purchasing in large quantities.

6. Going for multi-functional work equipment
   You will be able to achieve the minimalist and decluttered vibe for your home office if you forego owning a printer, a photocopier, and a scanner and opt to use a single machine that can perform all the different tasks instead.

7. Being clear about your work needs
   Avoid owning things for the sake of living up to expectations that you should have them. For instance, you may not really need paperclips, highlighters, rubber bands, a stapler, or a hole puncher for your work.

8. Letting go of knickknacks
   Those little trinkets cluttering your desk may be completely unnecessary, so get rid of them.

9. Making sure you have a clear desktop
   Your phone, computer, and inbox tray should be the only items perched on your work desk. Commit to having no papers (except those you are working on), pens, clips, stapler, and other desk junk.

10. Leaving the walls alone
    Avoid posting all sorts of things on your home office walls. It is better to leave the walls as is to steer clear of any visual

clutter. Make sure to remove any existing stuff on your walls. Some of those items, such as reference guides, can easily be saved on your computer.

11. Evaluating the contents of your drawers
Take the time to actually go through each one of them. Remove their contents, sort through, and get rid of those you no longer need. A drawer with pared down contents is much easier to open. Add dividers to help you assign a specific area for each item. It helps to immediately return the items you take out from the drawer to their exact spots.

12. Decluttering your computer desktop
Clear it of unnecessary icons. File away the icons you do need and call them up by making use of hotkeys instead.

13. Going for a minimalist desk
If you have no need of drawers, there is no reason why you cannot use a simple table as your work desk.

14. Clearing the floor
Commit to having just your work desk and chair on your home office floor. Avoid putting down files and boxes on it, ever. If you feel the need to place things everywhere, it might be due to your need for additional storage. Invest in a filing cabinet, organizers, and

drawers to make sure you have a designated place for all of your stuff.

15. Returning old files into storage
Signed contracts, leases, and other old files that you need to have a copy of but do not actually use that often can be boxed up and stored in the garage or attic.

## BATHROOM

<u>Declutter your bathroom by:</u>

1. Keeping only the products you regularly use
Although it is essential that you own first aid supplies, you are not necessarily icing bruises or sterilizing cuts on a daily basis. This is why you should sort your stuff, then separate the ones you use every day (toothbrush, toothpaste, shampoo, etc.) from those that you don't (pain medication). Transfer the second group of bathroom items to another spot in the closet.

2. Clearing out the medicine cabinet
You probably have worn-out scrunchies, bent hair pins, or expired medicine hiding in the medicine cabinet. Chuck these unnecessary items to reclaim the

space you need to store the stuff you do need.

3. Making use of a magnetic strip
   If you are currently storing your nail clippers, nail filers, bobby pins, and tweezers in jars that are placed on the bathroom sink, in a drawer, or inside the medicine cabinet, know that there is another way you could store these items while saving valuable space. Simply attach magnetic strips to the back of the medicine cabinet, then place your metal grooming items on the strips.

4. Filing your hair blower and straightening tools
   If you let them, your hair grooming tools can easily take over most of the space below your bathroom sink. Try attaching a magazine rack or file organizer behind a cabinet door or on one side of the bathroom sink, then store your hair dryer and other hair care tools inside. You may also buy an inexpensive bathroom organizer that you can get attached to your towel rack or mounted on the bathroom wall.

5. Keeping your brushes in Mason jars
   Mason jars are a godsend if you are looking for way to solve your storage issues with small bathroom items. You can use them to house your makeup

brush set, rest your toothbrush, and keep cotton balls.

6. Attaching a shelf above the bathroom door
The way you currently you store your towels is by attaching a row of hooks above the bathroom door. But there is a way for you to actually make more use of that space above the door, and that is to turn it into an additional storage unit. Use wooden screws to attach a couple of wooden shelf brackets onto each side of the bathroom door frame. Secure a shelf to these brackets, then add the extra soaps, shampoos, bath salts, toilet paper, and other items you want to store in there.

7. Placing a tension rod below the sink
Besides letting you hang your shower curtain in the bathroom, a tension rod can be used as a hanging place for your tile scrubbers, Windex, and other cleaning products. Simply attach it below your sink.

8. Adding tray organizers to your drawers
Instead of spending yet another ten minutes of your life in rummaging through the contents of your bathroom drawers to locate your lip balm, take steps to organize your stuff for good by

fitting a utensil tray or a divider inside the drawer.

9. Adding a spice rack to the wall
Secure a spice rack to that wall right next to the bathroom mirror. Use the additional space to store your collection of scrubs, sprays, gels, creams, and solutions.

<u>Give your bathroom a minimalist style by:</u>

1. Cutting back on the décor
Decorating your bathroom with seashells sounds cute, but it does not do anything to help you achieve the minimalist vibe you want your bathroom to exude. Your aim is to avoid using unnecessary décor in order to create a clean and simple space. Considering that the bathroom is usually one of a home's smallest rooms, it is important that you decide against using extra décor, which will only leave your bathroom looking cluttered and chaotic. Choose just one or two bathroom accessories that brings you the most delight and that will not cause surfaces to crowd.

2. Keeping all surfaces clear
It is best to make sure all the surfaces in your bathroom are kept clear and clutter-free. Seeing to it that you

accomplish this single thing is one of the most effective ways you can maintain your bathroom's decluttered and minimalist state.

3. Going all white
   Consider painting the walls in the bathroom an ivory shade, then hang up a white shower curtain in a sheer material. White surfaces never fail to instantly give a minimalist aesthetic to any room.

4. Keeping everything clean
   Fight the temptation to toss your clothes and towels on the bathroom floor. It helps to also give all of your bathroom surfaces, including the toilet, a quick wipe-down every day.

**DINING ROOM**

Declutter your dining room and give it the minimalist treatment by:

1. Clearing out your dining room storage units

   - Get rid of bent flatware, especially the ones that are so bent to the point that the sight of them on the dining table makes you embarrassed. Bent flatware should be disposed of if they could no longer be used.

- Throw out your <u>special occasion china</u>. It may be your most beautiful and sentimental possession, but it takes up too much valuable space if you only get to use it one to two times in a year. You could probably keep a single piece, one you may put on display. The rest are better off given to a relative who gets to use it more often.

- Tablecloths that are no longer usable should have no place in your minimalist and decluttered dining room. <u>Unusable tablecloths</u> include those that are stained, are covered with wax drippings, or are not the right size for your dining table. No matter the reason why you no longer find them useful, it is best for you to have them thrown out.

- Your collection of martini glasses may be the height of sophistication, but that is not worth anything if they are not ever used. <u>Specialty glassware</u>

also take up way too much space, which is why it is best if you simply picked one to 2 sets of glassware that you can commit to using on a frequent basis, then give away the rest.

- Some <u>mood lighting</u> goes a long way towards making dinnertime a more enjoyable experience. Steer clear of crazy-colored lighting; go for a slightly dimmed one that can transform a cafeteria-like meal into something you would eat in a cozy and intimate restaurant. Give up those bright, glaring lights you have in your dining room and replace them with dimmable bulbs.

- You do not have to hoard all the pieces included in a lovely centerpiece collection. Choosing to own <u>duplicate serving ware</u> will force you to sacrifice valuable space that would have served its purpose well for items that you actually need to have in your dining room. Downsize your collection of serving bowls, baskets, cheeseboards, and candlestick holders to only the most essential ones, and donate the duplicates to people who can use and enjoy them often.

- Although <u>single-use items</u> like disposable utensils, dishes, and serving ware can be convenient to use, they can out a big dent on your hosting budget and make a big impact on the environment. You are better off investing in a casserole dish, a carafe, salad tongs, and other high-quality yet affordable replacements.

- It is one thing to look back with great fondness on wonderful holiday gatherings or dinner parties you have experienced in the past, but is another thing to hold on to the party favors, personalized place cards, and other <u>old mementos</u> after all these years. Decide to keep one of each set, then let go of the rest.

- It might be best to place struggling indoor plants away from your dining room. Having them put on display where you and your family are trying to have your dinner is not conducive to eating. Place them somewhere else with better light instead.

2. Clearing out your dining table

- Make sure to stash your dining accessories instead of leaving them on your dining table. Keep the table clutter-free between meals by stowing the placemats, salt & pepper shakers, and napkin holder in a buffet or sideboard.

- Get smart with space. Avoid filling the dining room shelves, buffet, or sideboard with holiday decorations or fancy china you only get to use one a year. Consider transferring these items to another part of the house where you store your seldom-used belongings.

- Ensure your keys' safety by not tossing them on the dining table once you get home from work and designating them a place by the front door instead, such as an elegant dish or a row of hooks.

- Find another spot to place your electronic devices instead of letting them take up space on the dining table. This way, you won't have to be constantly gathering up your cell phones, chargers, and cords each time you need to set the table for dinner. Make sure to choose a convenient spot where your devices are safely out of the way.

- Relocate the laundry basket you have sitting there by the dining table. Stop treating your table as a folding station and invest in a tall cart or fold-down table you can use in the laundry area.

- Keep your kids belongings off the dining table. If they use it for doing their homework and craft projects, make sure to always clear off the dining table after they are done. Store the kids' school items in bins and baskets, ones that should be easy to pull out of your sideboard. If you would rather use the dining table for meals alone, consider setting up tables or desks in your kids' bedrooms.

- If your kids have taken to dropping their backpacks, sweaters, and jackets on the dining table, it may be necessary to give your entryway a makeover. You can have hooks installed by the front door to help keep backpacks and jackets from making their way into your dining room.

- Keep the junk mail, bills, and greeting cards from lording it over your dining table by setting up a convenient mail processing spot near the door. Consider investing in storage solutions that fit within furniture you already have in the dining room. A sideboard would be a great place to hold a basket for your mail, stamps, envelopes, and small file boxes.

- Give your magazines a good sorting if it has becomes home to piles of reading material. Decide on which issues are worth saving and should be discarded. Place the ones you want to save in a magazine holder parked in an ottoman with built-in storage or on a bookshelf.

3. Using appealing lighting fixtures
   To achieve a decluttered dining room that exudes a minimalist style, you might want to use a large pendant lamp

that instantly captivates anyone's attention. Doing so helps you ensure your dining room keeps its minimalist look without having it look boring and bare.

4. Making use of light colors
   Light-colored furniture made with natural materials would be great for your decluttered and minimalist dining room, since they give off that calming vibe to the space. And because they look good on their own, you would not need to bring in decorative accessories to make them shine.

5. Going for earthy tones
   You can try combining earthy colors with dark browns and gray accent pieces in order to highlight the elegance of your minimalist dining space.

6. Taking advantage of minimalist plants
   Minimalist plants make a nice addition to your dining room, with the way they easily make any room feel more natural and fresher. They are also perfect complements to furniture pieces that are made from wood, stone, and other natural materials. You can choose your kind of minimalist plant from the following:

- Cactus: This type of plant is the ideal plant to have in your dining room; except for its great need for plenty of water, it require very little in the maintenance department. Cactus plants are known for thriving with little care, making them one of the most favored indoor plants.

- Snake plant: The snake plant is known for its hardiness and clean lines, as well as its ability to withstand neglect. Snake plants can also benefit your health, as it functions as a natural air purifier to help improve the air quality in your home.

- Bird of Paradise: This minimalist plant is perfect for filling wide and tall spaces, especially those that are well-lit, making it an ideal houseplant to have inside your dining room. The Bird of Paradise is symmetrically shaped (in keeping with minimalist style), and shows off large canopy type leaves that are oval-shaped.

- Succulents: With their water retaining ability, succulents win hands-down as one of best minimalist plants to keep in your home. What is great about keeping succulents around in your space is the fact that even though they are low-maintenance, they pay their dues by injecting gorgeous hues to your minimalist dining room.

- Monstera: The Monstera plant, with its statement-making leaves, can thrive anywhere besides your dining room. Just make sure to place it in a spot that gets bright, indirect light to help make it grow faster. The only thing you have to take care of is to ensure this minimalist plant gets enough water to prevent its soil from drying out.

- String of Hearts: Also known as Sweetheart Vine, this flowering plant has little heart-shaped leaves growing from long, hanging vines that cascade down beautifully. Being semi-succulent, the String of Hearts plant can tolerate drought and a little direct sunlight.

7. Keeping your dining table neutral
While it can be argued that the table is your dining space's most significant

furniture piece, you may find yourself easily tempted to pick out one that you could call a statement piece. Instead of going for an ornately designed table, you may be better off keeping it neutral to make it more timeless and minimalist. It also helps to pay attention to construction quality when selecting your dining table. Great choices are wood, glass, stone, and other natural materials that gives you the freedom to change things up in the future if you need to.

## **LAUNDRY ROOM**

<u>Declutter your dining room and give it the minimalist treatment by:</u>

1. Recognizing that organization is key

   Keeping your laundry room organized is important, whether it is a corner space down in the basement or an airy showplace that boasts of plenty of storage, if you want to give it a minimalist and decluttered look and feel. Letting the space get overrun with clutter results in doing more difficult and longer laundry chores – and that is something that does not align with your desire to live minimally.

2. Taking out the trash
   Begin by looking for anything that needs to be thrown away in and around the workspace, washer, and dryer. You will be surprised by the number of bits and pieces you will find in these places that never found their way into the trash bin. Dispose of empty detergent containers, damaged laundry hampers, broken hangers, and expired laundry products. If you have never kept a trash can in your laundry room before, now is the time you should have one. You will need it for containing empty containers, pocket trash, and especially dryer lint filters, which need to be emptied after each load to help washed clothes dry faster as well as to prevent fires.

3. Tidying up the space
   Throw out anything that does not belong to the laundry room, such as garden tools, toys, and library books. If your laundry room happens to be a part of a multifunctional space, it is important to keep it clear of non-laundry related stuff. This is how you will be able to keep your clean clothes safe from soiling and cross-contamination issues from food or cleaning chemicals, have enough room for sorting and folding garments, and achieve the minimalist, uncluttered look you want to achieve.

4. Downsizing your laundry products
   You know you do not actually need to have 8 kinds of detergent products to clean your clothes. Stick to one product that helps you launder all types of fabrics instead of buying several specialty products. You might try washing your clothes with baking soda or adding distilled white vinegar for a better cleaning performance, as well as softening your clothes so that you no longer need to use dryer sheets or fabric softeners.

5. Creating a folding and clothesline space
   You do not need to toss all your washed clothes into the dryer. But instead of creating clutter by spreading them everywhere to let them dry naturally, you can designate an area to house a drying rack (wall-mounted or freestanding). You can also install a retractable clothesline that you can simply mount on one wall, and that you can easily keep put of the way when it is not used. Once you have already cleared out a space for letting your laundered clothes dry, find a spot to designate as your folding area, which can be a counter or a table. You can also use this spot for doing other laundry tasks, such as ironing clothes, so that you no longer have to bring in an ironing board.

6. Establishing a place to hold everything
   You could install storage shelves near the washer to hold your laundry products and other items that you would not want your kids and pets to get a hold of. You can also add more storage space to your laundry room by bringing in streamlined wall baskets and shelving units, which are especially handy for holding scrub brushes, scissors, clothespins, and other small laundry room items. A glass jar would be great for holding coins and other knickknacks you may find as you empty your clothes' pockets before adding them to the washer, while a basket will be useful for catching any single gloves or socks.

## **GARAGE**

<u>Turn your garage into a minimalist and decluttered space by:</u>

1. Having a fold-down table installed inside the garage
   This is a great way of gaining additional space in a rather tight garage. A fold-down table is designed to lay flush with your garage wall when it is not used to help clear up traffic zones. If you find the need for a surface to do some home repairs or to hold your potting plants,

you could easily fold out the table and lock it in a horizontal position.

1. Bringing in stackable storage drawers
   You can arrange several stackable storage drawers to make them fit any space in your garage. You can use them to hold toys, garden supplies, workshop tools, and other items that need to be stored in the garage. It is best to go for the ones made of a durable plastic material to help you view the contents inside while protecting them from dust.

2. Creating your own convenient storage unit
   You will be able make a convenient storage area for long, thin items like pipes, molding, and lightweight lumber with the use of rain gutters. You can get them inexpensively in aluminum or vinyl. Cut the sizes you prefer, then install by using screws in fastening their mounting brackets onto studs.

3. Storing your bike up and out of the way
   You can have your bicycles suspended from walls by using those simple clips you can buy from hardware stores. You might also try suspending them on sturdy racks, which are sold in closet accessory shops and bicycle stores. You can choose from among different designs, including shelves as well as

baskets that can hold water bottles, gloves, and helmets. Use screws in fastening the racks into the wall studs.

4. Corral your athletic gear
You can purchase shelves and racks at home centers and closet accessories shops. These items are designed to answer your storage issues with tennis rackets, baseball bats, basketballs, soccer balls, golf clubs, skis, in-line skates, and other types of sports equipment. You could also try making use of scrap lumber in making your own inexpensive storage unit that can be used to hold your sports equipment.

1. Make use of shelves and hooks for your various storage needs
Attach the shelves and hooks onto your garage door. They will allow you to store your family's protective gear next to their skateboards, roller blades, and bicycles.

2. Designate a spot for your sports and camping gear
The best place to assign as a storage area for your sports and camping gear would be near your car. You might also keep the equipment inside a storage chest that comes with wheels, making it easier for you to load and unload them.

3. Add a bench
   Placing a bench inside your garage helps you and your family have an area to put on as well as remove your sports gear. You can buy a bench that comes fitted with a shelf underneath, a perfect spot for letting your wet shoes and boots drain to dry. Otherwise, you can just put a plastic tray (choose one that is ridged) underneath the bench to achieve the same purpose.

## YARD

<u>Give a minimalist and decluttered look to your yard by:</u>

1. Paring down your ornaments
   You do not need to throw all of your lawn ornaments out, but you will be better off if you reduced the number of ornaments you have and you see to it that they are arranged in such a way that they look organized and clutter-free. You can try investing in lawn ornaments that also serve as useful gardening tools.

2. Rocking and rolling
   You will be surprised how easy it is to make your minimalist and decluttered yard look attractive just by the addition

of rocks to the space. It requires little maintenance to adorn your yard with rocks of various colors and sizes, especially if you add some succulents, moss, and other low-maintenance plants.

3. Going native when it comes to growing new plants
   This way, you are sure to have plants that do not require that much in terms of maintaining them. Native plants or flowers have natural resistance to pests and disease, do not need much water, and can easily adapt to your climate – all of which help you achieve the minimalist outdoor space you crave for.

4. Displaying simple furniture
   Go for neutral-colored furniture pieces that boast of simple, clean lines to complement beautifully with your pared-down lawn ornaments. You will be able to achieve your desired clutter-free, minimalist look effortlessly by choosing furniture pieces that are made with acacia and teak.

5. Making way for a minimalist garden
   Creating a minimalist garden does not mean putting up several tomato stakes in a plain yard and calling it a day. What you are going for is an outdoor space that is carefully cultivated, then adorned

with planters in streamlined, modern designs and complementary neutral colors.

# Chapter 6 Going Minimal With Social Media

To stay sane while living in today's hyperconnected, social media-driven world, it is important that you practice healthy habits that keep you from being controlled by technology. People are excessively plugged in, whether by getting a notification every time someone comments on your Instagram page or by scrolling incessantly through your Facebook feeds.

Cons of Constant Social Media Use
While all of this connectedness has its fair share of advantages, such as staying in touch with former classmates and long-lost relatives, being able to express what you want to say on your chosen platform, and making it easy for you to multitask, there are downsides to being too social media savvy:

- It may feel pleasurable to stare at your cellphone in the moment, but any pleasurable behavior can be addictive.

- The constant presence of electronics in people's lives nowadays, according to research, has caused the attention span of the average American to drop over the last ten years from twelve seconds down to eight, which is shorter than a goldfish's attention span.

- American Psychological Association reportedly found that technology has been pinpointed by almost twenty percent of the people they studied as a cause of stress.

- Being "always on" social media can also result in a number of physical ailments, including neck pain and high blood pressure.

Reasons to Wean Yourself Off Social Media
But going cold turkey with social media is not practical. The best route you can take towards freedom from possible social media addiction is by relaxing your hold on it (or is it the other way around?). When you do that, you will be able to reap the following benefits:

1. You get to escape from the constant onslaught of ads
   The idea that you could get addicted to the sensation of simply scrolling should be enough to alarm you. Keep in mind that the longer you remain on a site, the bigger the opportunity a company gains to show you ads. If you are going to live a

minimally and decluttered life, getting your vision and mind cluttered with ads day in, day out is not going to help at all.

2. Your constant fear of having missed out on something happening out there will decrease or go away
   You know that your family and friends can simply text you if they ever want to let you know about a gathering or get-together. And you can then make a decision later about wanting or not opting to joint an event. You can finally let go of that feeling that you are not in the loop regarding what is hot and what is not on TV right now, or who made to any of TC Candler's Top 100 Lists, whereas in the past you may have spent too much time updating yourself on all the latest TV shows or following numerous Instagram pages that you could no longer keep up with your household chores.

3. You will have one less item on your to-worry-over list
   The only time that getting on the social media bandwagon is beneficial for you is when you use it for making connections with people and for promoting your business. Otherwise, social media is just a huge waste of valuable time. When you go on a social media detox, you no longer worry over coming up with a classy clapback against a derogatory reply to

your latest heartfelt and personal tweet, or having to come up with new content for your Instagram stories to avoid losing your followers. You will not be worrying anymore about the dismal number of likes you recently received and you will never have to deal with all the stress that brings.

Signs of Social Media Downward-Spiral
The following are signs that a social media detox is in order:
- "Stressed out" is your name when you cannot locate your smartphone
- After you are done using social media, you somehow feel anger, anxiety, or depression
- You have this fear of missing anything and everything if you stop checking your phone
- Staying up late or getting up earlier than usual is how you end up because you are tinkering with the phone
- Checking your phone every minute or so is a compulsion you find so hard to resist
- Being preoccupied with the number of likes and comments your social media posts collect has become as normal as breathing air
- You find it hard to concentrate on anything if you cannot check your phone

Breaking Away from Technology Toxicity
Enjoy a minimalist relationship with social media with these tips:

1. Go slow in changing your digital habits
   Give yourself a bit of a leeway when it comes to making over your technology habits. It could be only checking your social media feed every three hours, turning your cell phone off one hour before going to bed, or banning all gadgets from the dining room. Pick one habit to change first, seeing to it that you will stick to changing it within one to two weeks no matter what happens. Once done, you can then move on to changing another digital habit.

2. Come up with a gadget list
   Prior to committing yourself to a digital detox, consider making up two lists. One list will show all the gadgets that are in your possession, reflecting your dependence on technology. The second list will show the activities you enjoy the most doing, but are unable to do at present. Making up the two lists will force you to face the fact that cutting down on your use of digital devices will be the way you could regain the hours to spend on things that hold more meaning in your life than updating your Facebook status by the hour.

3. Let yourself have a daily time allowance
   Putting in place a daily time allowance in using your devices is an effective way of making sure you will stick to your digital detox endeavors. This could be anywhere from fifteen minutes to two hours, but it is important for you to recognize how differently you feel during the time frame that you are not falling down the rabbit hole of social media. Distract yourself during that period of social media fast by doing something enjoyable but completely unrelated to using gadgets. Cutting back on the time you spend on your devices helps you focus more on what is happening out there in the real world. This is also a great way to encourage yourself to have more in-person interactions with other people instead of constantly communicating with others through a cellphone or computer screen.

4. Transfer your social media to another screen
   While this is a temporary solution, all that extra swiping may get you discouraged enough to actually stall your unhealthy fixation with social media.

5. Turn your bedroom space into a no-tech sanctuary

You probably use your cellphone as your handheld alarm clock, but every time you reach for that contraption so you could shut it off, it is so easy to begin scrolling through your social media feeds. This is why it is best not to bring your cellphone inside your bedroom during nighttime. Buy yourself an alarm clock so you can actually sleep much better.

6. Turn off your notifications
   Being constantly updated with all that is happening around the word is great, but not if it is always distracting you from the important things you are doing at the moment. You will never get anything done if you are interrupted by push notifications every thirty minutes.

7. Never use your cellphone when eating
   Smartphones gleaming right next to the plates is a common sight nowadays, whether it is in the restaurant or at home. But research has demonstrated that the mere presence of your cellphone on the table while you are in a convo, even if you are not actually checking it, can negatively affect how you interact with other people. It is as if your brain is waiting for your cellphone to light up and show the latest notifications, and this keeps you from being fully present in the moment, which is contrary to the minimalist and

decluttered way of life you are trying to uphold.

8. Maintain your minimalist social media lifestyle
    - Stop clicking Like. You may use social media as a way of connecting and staying in touch with your loved ones. But you do not owe it to anybody to click Like or to be available all the time.
    - Enjoy some time all by yourself. Instead of feeling left out, consider going out for a solitary walk or reading a book.
    - Try leaving your phone at home whenever you have to go out for quick errands.
    - Delete all of your phone's social media apps to curb easy access and temptation.
    - Treat using your social media as a professional obligation.
    - Enlist the support of your family and friends in your social media minimalism journey.
    - Take up exercise or some other fun way to distract yourself.
    - Go out on dinner date with friends.
    - Monitor your progress by journaling your thoughts and experience.

# Chapter 7 Guide to Financial Minimalism

Practicing minimalism in your life does not prevent you from spending money. Rather, it steers you towards spending your money on the few things that truly matter to you. Minimalism changes your money mindset from constantly finding ways to make money to using your money to live your life enjoyably.

What it all boils down to is that minimalism helps you manage your finances. Below are the various ways a minimalist lifestyle helps you avoid financial distress:

1. Lets you prioritize your spending
   By embracing minimalism in your life, you also embrace those things that matter most to you, a fact that inevitably affects how you go about your finances, especially with regards to spending your money. It is only natural that how you part with your money will change if you are not hung up on owning certain items and focus more instead on acquiring specific experiences. Being able to discover the most important things in your life encourages you to set your spending priorities straight, ultimately

changing your way of handling your finances in general.

2. Puts a limit on your need for possessions
Be being focused on applying minimalism to the different aspects of your life, you end up limiting your belongings. Because you choose to either own fewer possessions or spend a lower amount when purchasing things, you force yourself to decide on whether you should watch your savings soar by reducing your spending or get your debts settled. What usually happens is that because you are no longer buying as much as before, you end up directing more money into your other financial goals that enable you to spend more on experiences instead of things.

3. Helps you save more on rent or mortgage
When you decide to live minimally, you no longer need as much room for storing all the things you have acquired through the years. If you are renting or buying a smaller space, you are able to save on rent payment, but you still get to realize your dream of living in a nice house that has clean lines as well as a space you absolutely love. This way, you save not only on your rent or mortgage, but on your utilities as well.

4. Teaches you to become mindful with your budget and financial goals

Practicing mindfulness is involved when you apply minimalism to your life, and it benefits you as you establish your financial goals and start budgeting, which is your spending plan in accordance with your current financial priorities. In the process of discovering the things that you believe are the most important, you will find it less difficult to make up your mind about how and when you should be spending your money. You will also discover aspects where a change will have to be made in how you handle your finances, such as the amount you set aside for paying in monthly interest on different loans.

5. Helps you manage your debts
   One of the most effective ways you can simplify your finances is concentrating on settling your debts. You could start by paying off your consumer debt, then using just one credit card in handling emergencies. You can achieve financial freedom once you are able to eliminate your debt – you could take a few months off from work in order to travel, or you could just leave your job altogether to pursue your passions. When you never have to think about additional monthly obligations, you will find it easier to discover the things that matter most to you.

6. Allows you to make money off your clutter
   At the beginning stage of your journey in embracing minimalism, you may decide to sell some of your belongings that are no longer necessary in your life. You can then utilize the money you make in clearing off your debt and other financial issues cluttering up your life. Another way you could make use of that money is for starting an emergency fund or for funding the destination trip of your dreams.

7. Allows you to simplify your finances
   Going minimal with your finances could mean paying all of your bills in one day, using cash to purchase your everyday needs (making it easy for you to monitor your spending), and using an app for simplifying the process of budgeting (just enter your purchases to get updated on where you stand with your financial goals and limits).

8. Makes giving back easier
   Knowing what you believe is the most important and getting a grip on your finances makes it easier for you to give back, whether through donations or in time. Living minimally allows you to identify what and how much you are able to give, and makes it less difficult for you to shift priorities as needed.

Practicing financial minimalism is as easy as following these tips:

1. Give your money mindset a makeover
   Stop thinking up ways to borrow money, and focus instead on actually owning the things you have. This means letting go of the mindset that you own something in terms of how much and how long you will be paying for it. You might say you purchased that car because you of the great deal you were offered on the lease, and you only had to pay two hundred fifty dollars each month. Your goal may be to stretch out your finances to the point where you are sure you will be making the lowest payments possible, which allows you to live a lifestyle that you believe you deserve but are unable to afford. By following a minimalist budget, you turn things around and think in terms of owning your possessions rather than paying for them for a certain period of time. Forget about asking how much the monthly payment will be; instead, you should be asking about the actual cost if you purchased an item right then and there.

2. Identify your money values and priorities
   To eliminate the things that are not essential in your life, you have to determine which things are necessary to you and which are not. Doing so will help

you figure out your financial values in order to set up your financial priorities.

- Your financial values might include:
    - Putting 20 percent of your income into savings
    - Setting aside 30 percent of a buffer for your income versus expenses
    - Living a life that is free from debts
    - Retiring before 60
    - Donating 10 percent of your income to your church

- You can put your financial priorities in place once you have spelled out your financial values in definite terms. When you really think about it, your financial priorities will be the basis of your financial goals in life. Being the plan you will use to get yourself from your current situation to where you aspire to be, your financial priorities will change as your financial circumstances also change.

- Your financial priorities may include any or all of the following:
    - Finish paying all debts, such as auto loans, student loans,

- and credit cards, within three years
- As soon as debts are paid off, start putting aside 20 percent of income as savings
- Begin donating 10 percent of income to church
- Earning 20 percent more income through a job on the side
- Preparing a financial plan for the long term that allows retiring before age 60

3. Evaluate your consumption by listing your spending habits
   Write down all your expenses, making sure to make your list as detailed as possible. Remember to include everything you spend your money on, such as wedding gifts, travel expenses, and trips to Target. Once you are done with your list, check each item as you ask yourself whether the item has brought value to your life and has helped you meet your financial priorities. You may be surprised to find that you are spending your money on certain expenses that are not in keeping with your financial goals. You should then cross these items off your minimalist budget.

4. Pare down your accounts
   You have a messy problem in your hands if you are juggling more than eight accounts, using one for down payment savings, one for taxes, one for your emergency fund, one for vacations, and so on. This can easily lead you to using one account to fund another, especially if you are stuck in making multiple payments to different places.
   - The minimalist budget depends on just one primary checking account as well as one primary savings account. You should be using your savings account in securing your emergency fund, and your checking account should be handling your non-discretionary expenses (bills, housing, debt) and discretionary expenses (entertainment).
   - Limit yourself to just one credit card or none at all. You may regret the fact that you could no longer enjoy the rewards, but you will reap far more benefits in simplifying your finances and getting organized with your spending.

5. Establish your spending plan
   This is the first thing you have to sort out if you want your minimalist lifestyle to be successful. Your net take-home pay is the actual figure reflected on your check. You

should then compute your fixed monthly expenses, which can include the following:
- Water, electricity, gas, garbage, and other utilities
- Rent
- Auto maintenance and gasoline
- Kids' education and activities
- Retirement accounts and other savings
- Groceries
- Internet and cell phone
- Medical expenses and health insurance
- Car insurance

6. Get your payments automated
When you decide to practice minimalism with your finances, it only makes sense to automate your payments as much as you can. You can also automate:
    - Your bill payments
    - Your savings by having it directly deposited into your retirement accounts
    - Your debt payments by having them auto-debited every first day of the month

7. Be critical of all your future purchases
Always remember that it takes a lot of time and effort to earn your money, which is why you need to ensure that each item you buy is definitely spending your hard-

earned money on. You can accomplish that by asking yourself the following before any purchase:

- *Is it something I can really afford?*
  You have to determine first if you have the resources to pay for the item. If it is something you cannot afford, purchasing it will likely cause you to go into debt. In addition to that, you want to make sure the money spent on this item is not going to prevent you from buying another item that you actually need.

- *What will I use it for?*
  What do you plan on doing with your new purchase? Dig deep into the ways it adds value to your life. Think about whether or not it will help you reach a specific goal.

- *Will I use this often?*
  You should also have a good idea regarding how often the item is going to be used. Buying something does not really make sense if you know you will only be using it one to two times. It is important to be honest with yourself while figuring out the potential number of times you are likely to put an item to use. For instance, you may surely use a

coffee maker on a daily basis, so it would be sensible to buy it instead of purchasing a blender that you may set aside after using it just a few times.

- *Do I want this item?*
  Be clear about your reason for wanting to have the item in the first place. You probably just want to buy it because your brother also has it or you only want to impress a neighbor. Seriously question your motives and determine if you want the item with all your heart or if you merely want to have something new to show off to friends.

# Chapter 8 Embracing the Minimalist Diet

To embrace the minimalist diet is to use a pared-down approach in preparing and cooking your nutritionally-balanced meals, as well as making the most of your ingredients so that you are able to use as few as possible without sacrificing the quality and quantity of your foods. Following a minimalist diet encourages you to be intentional in the way the meals you prepare fit your lifestyle while approaching it in the manner that works for you.

Heed the following tips on giving the minimalist diet a go:

1.  Adopt a meal plan that works for you
    Consider following a meal plan in which you commit to eating the same foods constantly. Going this route enables you to save money by not relying on exotic ingredients, new spices, or a wide array of grocery items.

    - Make sure to have the right staples on hand in order for you to whip up easy-to-create and time-saving meals such as burritos, vegan sandwiches, chickpea and sweet

potato curry, breakfast muesli, and smoothies.
- Try preparing your own nourish bowls, which can be an effective way to make use of leftovers, by simply tossing your preferred grain, beans or another type of protein, hummus, vegetables, and avocado into a bowl.
- When starting out, it helps to evaluate your favorite meals and take note of the ingredients needed to prepare them. Once you are done making a list of our most preferred dishes, check out which of their ingredients overlap. Pick out the dishes that require the same ingredients to help you make the most of your go-to-recipes while using the least quantity of ingredients.

2. Keep it simple when it comes to snacking

Practicing the minimalist diet is a great way to give your snacking habits a makeover if you are a huge snacker that cannot get enough of junk food and other heavily processed snacks. Decide on minimizing your snacking habit so that you are doing it less often. Stick to healthy, filling snacks like salads, cheese sticks, jerky, fresh fruit, dried fruit, apple slices with peanut butter, and veggies with hummus. See to it that your snacks are focused on whole ingredients as much as possible. This not only helps improve your overall health, but helps you save money as well.

3. Go for themed nights
   Themed nights is an easy way to make sure you are following a minimalist diet while keeping things from becoming too repetitive and unexciting. Try having your own version of a Meatless Monday or Taco Tuesday, which is an enjoyable way of introducing your kids to a simplified, healthy way of eating. What is great about going for themed nights is that you are encouraged to place a limit on your shopping and you will know exactly what you need to buy so you are not walking around the store aimlessly and snatching up food items that are not minimalist diet-friendly.

4. Ensure your nutrition
   Following the minimalist diet works most effectively when you use whole ingredients in cooking your meals and snacks. Make sure to concentrate on getting your body's nutritional needs from fresh vegetables and fruits, legumes and beans, and whole grains. To make sure you are getting your ingredients near the source, consider growing your own vegetables at home. Otherwise, try to purchase your fresh produce in farmers'

markets, whole grain breads in local bakeries, and dried beans and whole grain pasta in bulk stores. Making a variety of minimalist diet meals is easy and possible when you constantly have your food staples on hand.

5. Stock up on ingredients in your minimalist pantry
   Avoid keeping multiples of each of your ingredients on hand. Keep in mind that sales in stores occur every six weeks, eliminating the need for you to hoard dozens of each ingredient.
   Make sure your pantry constantly has the following staple foods:

   - Dry goods – These items form the basis of your minimalist diet-friendly pantry. They are not only the perfect base of many nutritious meals, but they also keep well for longer and do not cost that much.
     - Lentils and beans – dried green lentils, dried red lentils, dried chickpeas, dried split peas, canned brown lentils, canned black beans, canned kidney beans, and canned chickpeas
     - Grains – quinoa, oats, barley, bulgur, couscous, brown rice, white rice, long pasta (spaghetti, linguine,

fettuccine), short pasta (penne, macaroni, rotini), and lasagna
- Nuts and seeds – almonds, peanuts, chia seeds, sunflower seeds, pumpkin seeds, and trail mix
- Dried fruit – raisins, craisins, and dates
- Canned foods – tomato sauce, coconut milk, canned tomatoes, canned applesauce, canned fruit (peaches, pears, pineapple), and canned fish (tuna, salmon, sardines)
- Other dry goods – crackers, cornmeal, popcorn kernels, breakfast cereals, cornstarch, dark chocolate, and peanut butter

- Oils and vinegars – These inexpensive yet versatile items are primarily used in seasoning and cooking meals.
  - Olive oil – for low-heat cooking and salads preparation
  - Flavored oils – coconut oil, garlic oil, sesame oil, and chili oil
  - Neutral cooking oils – Avocado oil, sunflower oil,

and canola oil (for baking and other high-heat cooking methods)
  - White vinegar
  - Flavored vinegars – apple cider and red wine

- Baking supplies – These are items that may be optional, although having sugar, all-purpose flour, and baking soda is recommended as many recipes usually call for them.
  - All-purpose flour and whole wheat flour
  - Brown sugar, white sugar, and powdered sugar
  - Baking soda and baking powder
  - Vanilla extract
  - Cocoa powder
  - Unsweetened shredded coconut
  - Chocolate chips

- Herbs and spices – Avoid creating clutter in the cupboard by only stocking up on spices and herbs that you use on a regular basis, and only in quantities that you will use up. Take your pick from the following:
  - Black pepper and white pepper

- Oregano
- Chili flakes
- Salt
- Curry powder
- Chili powder
- Paprika
- Ginger
- Turmeric
- Cinnamon
- Nutmeg
- Cayenne
- Thyme
- Basil
- Cloves

6. Cook minimalist meals from scratch
Cooking a simple, nutritious, and delicious dish is not based on how many ingredients or gadgets are used in preparing it. Give the following recipes, one for each day of the week, a try:

- <u>Classic Chicken Mushroom Burgers</u>

  *Ingredients*: Chopped & rinsed mushrooms (1 pack), chopped & rinsed spinach (1 cup), ground lean chicken (1 pound), olive oil (2 tablespoons), chopped & rinsed yellow/red onion (1/4 piece), salt, and black pepper

*Directions*: Pat dry the mushrooms, spinach, and onion. Add to a skillet filled with oil and heated on medium. Sauté with pepper and salt. Once veggies are tender, stir in ground chicken. Mold into patties and place on a foil-lined baking sheet. Broil on each side for five minutes or until golden brown.

- Basic Black Bean Soup

    *Ingredients*: Black beans (15 ½ ounces), diced tomatoes (15 ounces), and chicken broth (1 cup)

    *Directions*: Fill a medium pot with all ingredients. Heat to boiling, then let mixture simmer for ten minutes. Turn off heat before processing with a hand blender.

- Beef Stew

    *Ingredients*: Chopped mixed veggies (2 cups), baked sweet potato (1 piece), ground beef (4 ounces), olive oil (1 teaspoon), and chopped garlic (1/2 teaspoon)

    *Directions*: Add oil to a saucepan heated on medium. After one minute, turn heat down to low. Stir in garlic to cook for two minutes. Stir in vegetables; once softened, add ground beef and cook until browned through. Serve beef stew with baked sweet potato.

- <u>Grilled Cheese & Turkey Sandwich</u>

  *Ingredients*: Sliced fresh turkey (2 ounces), sprouted grain bread (2 slices), tomato slices (2 pieces), sliced cheddar cheese (1 ounce), and pesto (1 teaspoon)

  *Directions*: Mist cooking spray onto a preheated grill pan. Smear each slice of bread with pesto. Top one bread piece with turkey, cheese, tomatoes, and remaining bread. Place on the grill pan to cook for two minutes on each side.

- <u>Chicken Tenders</u>

  *Ingredients*: Egg (1 piece), wheat germ (1 piece), 1-oz. chicken cutlet strips (6 pieces), and panko breadcrumbs (1 cup)

  *Directions*: Combine wheat germ and breadcrumbs. Dip chicken strips in egg before coating with breadcrumbs mixture. Place on a parchment-lined pan and bake at

375 degrees Fahrenheit for eight minutes.

- <u>Easy Parchment Baked Salmon</u>

  *Ingredients*: Salmon fillet (1 piece), lemon slices (2 pieces), Dijon mustard (2 teaspoons), soy sauce (1 teaspoon), and parchment paper (1 large square)

  *Directions*: Place salmon on left side of parchment. Spread mustard on top before drizzling with soy sauce. Top with lemon slices and cover with right side of parchment. Seal by rolling tightly at the edges. Bake at 375 degrees Fahrenheit for twelve minutes.

- <u>Ginger Mushrooms</u>

  *Ingredients*: Freshly grated ginger (2 teaspoons), thickly sliced shiitake mushrooms (8 ounces), toasted sesame seeds (1 tablespoon), sesame oil (2 teaspoons), grated garlic cloves (2 pieces), and coarsely chopped watercress (1 bunch)

  *Directions*: Stir garlic and ginger into oil heated on medium-low. After two minutes, turn heat up to medium and stir in mushrooms. After cooking for four minutes, stir in watercress. Cook for two to three minutes more before sprinkling sesame seeds on top.

- <u>Parmesan Halibut</u>

    *Ingredients*: Skinless halibut filet (4 ounces), olive oil (2 teaspoons), dried oregano (1/4 teaspoon), chili pepper flakes (1/4 teaspoon), trimmed Brussels sprouts (1 cup), grated Parmesan (3 tablespoons), and lemon wedge (1 piece)

    *Directions*: Toss oil, salt, and black pepper with Brussels sprouts. Spread into a single layer in a cooking spray-misted baking dish. Bake for twenty minutes at 400 degrees Fahrenheit. Coat filet with oil, then rub all over with mixed oregano and cheese (2 tablespoons). Lower oven temperature at 375 degrees Fahrenheit, toss the sprouts with remaining Parmesan, and move to the side of the baking dish. Add the halibut to the other side and bake for ten minutes. Toss chili pepper flakes and lemon juice with the sprouts and serve.

- <u>Tarragon Mustard Chicken</u>

  *Ingredients*: Chicken breasts (4 pieces), salt, pepper, half-and-half (1/3 cup), chopped fresh tarragon (3 teaspoons), olive oil (1 tablespoon), chicken stock (1/2 cup), and Dijon mustard (1 tablespoon)

  *Directions*: Heat olive oil on medium-high in a large saucepan. Season chicken breasts with salt and pepper, then add to the oil and sauté for ten minutes. Transfer browned chicken to a plate and keep warm by tenting with foil. Pour chicken stock into pan and cook for two to three minutes or until reduced to half its original volume. Whisk in half-and-half, mustard, tarragon, and chicken juices; cook for two minutes more before serving with chicken pieces drizzled with sauce.


- <u>Lime Chicken Bowls</u>

  *Ingredients*: Cubed chicken breasts (3 pounds), red wine vinegar (3 tablespoons), chili powder (2 teaspoons), garlic powder (1 teaspoon), cracked pepper (1/4 teaspoon), olive oil (6 tablespoons), fresh lime juice (1/4 cup), paprika (1 teaspoon), and kosher salt (1 teaspoon)

*Directions*: Mix together olive oil, pepper, vinegar, salt, paprika, lime juice, garlic powder, and chili powder. Slice chicken into cubes before tossing with the marinade. Refrigerate for two hours. Add marinated chicken to a baking sheet and bake at 400 degrees Fahrenheit for twenty minutes.

- Cashew Alfredo Butternut Squash Noodles

*Ingredients*: Raw cashews (2 cups), minced garlic cloves (2 pieces), salt (3/4 teaspoon), Dijon mustard (1 teaspoon), fresh lemon juice (3 tablespoons), diced onion (1/2 piece), unsweetened almond milk (1 ¼ cups), black pepper (1/4 teaspoon), spiralized butternuts squash (8 cups)

*Directions*: Place cashews in water (3 cups) and let soak overnight; drain well and set aside. Heat a large saucepan on medium. Add garlic and onion and sauté for two minutes. Place drained cashews in a blender; add cooked onion-garlic mixture, salt, lemon, almond milk, and mustard and process until smooth and creamy. Saute butternut squash in same pan for ten minutes. Toss with Alfredo sauce and serve immediately.

- <u>Yummy Chicken Lettuce Cups</u>

  *Ingredients*: Whole rotisserie chicken (1 piece), thin red pepper slices (1 cup), shredded carrots (1 cup), sliced avocado (1 piece), Lettuce (2 heads), lemon dressing (2 tablespoons), and prepared tabouleh salad (2 cups)

  *Directions*: Discard the skin from the chicken. Shred meat with a fork or slice into cubes. Add lemon dressing to the shredded veggies and toss to combine. Add all ingredients to the lettuce leaves and serve right away.

- <u>Sunshine Egg Muffins</u>

  *Ingredients*: Eggs (6 pieces), cooked chopped spinach (1/2 cup), shredded cheddar cheese (1/3 cup), salt (1/4 teaspoon), pepper (1/4 teaspoon), crumbled cooked bacon

(1/3 cup), diced tomatoes (1 tablespoon), and chopped fresh parsley (1 tablespoon)

*Directions*: Line a 6-cup muffin tin with parchment and set oven at 375 degrees Fahrenheit to preheat. Whisk eggs until smooth, then mix with cheese, bacon, and spinach. Pour into muffin cups and bake for fifteen to eighteen minutes. Serve right away.

- <u>Pork Sausage Burritos</u>

  *Ingredients*: Pork sausage (1/2 pound), large eggs (6 pieces), medium-size tortillas (8 pieces), cooked chopped potatoes (2 cups), half-and-half (2 tablespoons), and shredded cheese (3/4 cup)

  *Directions*: Cook pork sausage in skillet heated on medium; transfer to a plate lined with paper towels. Add potatoes to the same pan and toss for two minutes or until heated through; set aside on a plate. Melt butter (1 tablespoon) in the same skillet. Add a mixture of eggs whisked with salt, pepper, and half-and-half. Cook until set to preferred texture and set aside on a plate. Fill tortillas with eggs, sausage, potatoes, and cheese. Roll up to form burritos and serve.

- <u>Steak Salad</u>

*Ingredients*: Flank steak (1 pound), ground black pepper (1/2 teaspoon), red wine vinegar (1 ½ tablespoons), skin-on wedged red potatoes (4 pieces), halved grape tomatoes (1 cup), salt (1/2 teaspoon), olive oil (2 tablespoons), Dijon mustard (1 tablespoon), trimmed green beans (1/2 pound), and sliced pitted Kalamata olives (1/4 cup)

*Directions*: Mist cooking spray onto a broiler pan and preheat the broiler. Rub black pepper and salt all over the flank steak before adding to broiler pan. Broil on each side for three minutes, then slice thinly into strips after allowing to rest on a cutting board for five to ten minutes. Fill a pot with the potatoes, then add cold water to cover potatoes by one inch. Heat to boiling, cook for eight to ten minutes, remove by using a slotted spoon, and set aside. Fill same pot with the green beans, boil for three to five minutes, drain well, and rinse under cool water. Whisk together the mustard, vinegar, and olive oil, then add two-thirds of the mixture to the potatoes before tossing gently. Place the steak, green beans, potatoes, olives, and tomatoes on your serving platter. Serve drizzled with the remaining dressing.

7. Learn the art of meal prepping
Meal prepping is a minimalist approach to making homemade meals that are so delicious that you will not get tired of eating them every day. What is great about meal prepping is that you are not required to buy expensive tools or do some complicated planning in order to yield impressive dishes. What you only have to provide is your effort and time. Not only will meal prepping enable you to save time, but it also helps you reduce waste and save money.

- Meal prepping comes in four types:
  - Single-serve meals: This type of meal prepping will have you preparing food that is usually enough for a few days of consumption, and then portioning it into single-serving containers.

- Complete make-ahead meals: Here you will be preparing an entire meal, after which you will keep it in the refrigerator or freezer.

- Batch cooking/freezing: Prepare multiple meals, portion them, and store in the freezer. This method is great for large pots of mashed sweet potatoes, rice, soup, or other recipes that can easily be cooked in big amounts.

- Ingredient prep: This type or meal prepping is perfect for you love cooking and serving dishes all at once. All you have to do is prep the different parts of recipes. You will be able to save time once you are all set to cook because you have already marinated the meat, combined the spices, or chopped the veggies ahead of time.

- Do not complicate things: As a beginner in meal prepping, it helps to keep things simple at the start. You can choose to concentrate on a single main dish or prepare a couple of one-pot recipes. Make sure to keep yourself from being preoccupied for an entire day in cooking complicated dishes. If things get too elaborate, you may find meal prepping to be a difficult task and have second thoughts about doing it all over again. Stick to prepping only one recipe during your first attempts, then explore additional recipes once you get the hang of it.

- Cook the dishes you actually want to eat: There is no need for you to immediately branch out to exotic dishes, especially if you make sure that your chosen meal prep recipes are balanced. Give yourself time to work with recipes you really love, or you may just end up wasting food, time, and effort.

- Set aside time for prepping your meals: Meal prepping is not possible without prep time, so ensure setting aside 1 to 2 days every week for prepping dishes. You will be surprised by how much time can be cut down if you try multitasking a bit (for example, using both the stovetop and oven to prep two to three dishes at the same time). In times like these, you may find it convenient to use an air fryer or an Instant Pot. Keep in mind that your best schedule for meal prepping is the schedule that works for your lifestyle, so it is up to you if you want to prep on Saturdays only or every Tuesday and Thursday.

- Prepare meals in the amount that is enough for you: See to it that you prep enough dishes to suit your eating plan. Work around your schedule, since work lunches, happy hours, and other inevitable events may get in the way with mealtimes. Really think about whether or not you have to meal prep every single day, or just enough to last you a couple of days.

- Keep things interesting: You will save lots of time by prepping the same meal day after day, which is so minimalist, but it can lead to boredom. If eating the same dish over and over is not your cup of tea, try making little adjustments to how you prep to ensure you end up with a different dish each time. For instance, keep meals interesting by swapping in various sauces, garnishes, or veggies for each food container. On the other hand, you might consider prepping and freezing several recipes ahead of time. During the next several days, you can then just let 1 or 2 containers thaw in the fridge each day, ensuring that you can enjoy various meals throughout the week.

- Make sure to prep balanced meals: Plan meals that still satisfy your taste buds while you take into consideration your health goals and diet needs. You may find it a breeze to prepare a large bowl of butternut squash chowder for dinner, but you know it hardly qualifies as a complete and satisfying meal. This is why you need to include some protein, a few carbohydrates, and plenty of healthy fats into your meal planning.

- Use quality food keepers: Keep your meal-prep dishes hot or cold by using high-quality storage containers. Consider investing in thermal containers, which are made of stainless steel and do a great job keeping cooked food chilled or warm. You can also use glassware, which is the safest to use and is best for enjoying cold meals.

# Chapter 9 Adopting a Minimalist and Clutter-Free Wardrobe

Adopting a minimalist wardrobe may be the easiest aspect of your life in which to start practicing the minimalist way of living. The reality is that the more clothes you own, the less you actually get to enjoy them. You probably find yourself constantly wondering why, after having filled all corners and spaces in your closet with enough clothes to literally last you a lifetime, you still end up having nothing to wear.

By embracing minimalism in building your wardrobe, you reap the joy of investing in possessions that you love and deciding to stop accumulating things you simply like. Having fewer choices actually forces your mind to be in positive mode.

Aside from giving you that wonderful feeling you get, every single day, when you are wearing something special, a minimalist wardrobe also provides the following benefits:

- You will become the proud owner of a decluttered closet. Digging through clothes you rarely or never wear will already become a thing of the past.
- You will have extra money and time on your hands for more important things. Because you are already contented with what you have in your minimalist wardrobe, you are shopping less often than you used to and are spending less money on clothes.
- You will be making a positive impact on the environment. In the United States alone, thirteen million tons of textiles are disposed of, which can be reduced if people commit to buying and wearing only long-wear clothing rather than going for fast fashion garments.
- You will gain extra confidence in yourself. Because you know that all the clothes in your minimalist wardrobe are your best ones, you feel great about yourself no matter what you throw on yourself.

Adopting a minimalist wardrobe may be the easiest aspect of your life in which to start practicing the minimalist way of living. The reality is that the more clothes you own, the less you actually get to enjoy them. You probably find yourself constantly wondering why, after having filled all corners and spaces in your closet with enough clothes to literally last you a lifetime, you still end up having nothing to wear.

By embracing minimalism in building your wardrobe, you reap the joy of investing in possessions that you love and deciding to stop accumulating things you simply like. Having fewer choices actually forces your mind to be in positive mode.

Aside from giving you that wonderful feeling you get, every single day, when you are wearing something special, a minimalist wardrobe also provides the following benefits:

- You will become the proud owner of a decluttered closet. Digging through clothes you rarely or never wear will already become a thing of the past.
- You will have extra money and time on your hands for more important things. Because you are already contented with what you have in your minimalist wardrobe, you are shopping less often than

you used to and are spending less money on clothes.
- You will be making a positive impact on the environment. In the United States alone, thirteen million tons of textiles are disposed of, which can be reduced if people commit to buying and wearing only long-wear clothing rather than going for fast fashion garments.
- You will gain extra confidence in yourself. Because you know that all the clothes in your minimalist wardrobe are your best ones, you feel great about yourself no matter what you throw on yourself.

<u>Begin building your minimalist wardrobe by following these steps:</u>

1. Lay down the foundation

    - Determine your lifestyle: You need to be truly aware of who you are, where you live, what you do for a living, and what your life goals are in order to figure out what you really need in your wardrobe. For instance, if you live in a hot-climate location, owning gloves and scarves will be useless. If you have never been accused of being a gym rat and have no plans of turning into one soon, then you can go ahead and donate the cute pair of sports shoes hiding at the back of the closet for two years.

- Know your personal style: It is time for you to focus on style once you have the practical considerations nailed down. Pay attention to your favorite outfits as well as those you that required you to part with a large amount of money. Really see the signs of your personal style – maybe you favor neutrals over vibrant colors, feel most beautiful in an all-black outfit, or would rather slouch comfortably in your favorite t-shirt, jeans, and sneakers combo than to stride uncertainly in strappy heels while wearing a slinky dress. Whatever you feel is your true personal style, make it the basis of your minimalist outfits.

- Consider your laundry situation: You may feel in your heart that expensive suits are the embodiment of your style, but if you cannot even afford to have them dry-cleaned, then you have to think twice about making them the anchor of your minimalist wardrobe. Avoid buying sequined garments if hand-washing is not your thing. Keep in mind that minimalism is all about simplifying your life and making it more enjoyable, so choose outfits that suit your routine as well as your aesthetic.

- Nail down your color palette: Doing so helps you become more adept at mixing and matching your pieces. Make sure a major part of your minimalist wardrobe can work with other pieces in putting together an outfit. It helps to select a color palette that goes perfectly with your personal style.

- Let go of some of your clothes: Part with any clothing that does not fit your body properly, makes you recall bad memories, or does not match with anything else in your closet. But do not just toss these items into a landfill; instead:

  - Donate the clothes you do not intend to keep to your friends, the Salvation Army, or Goodwill.

  - Sell to thrift stores, many of which are owned independently and are willing to offer you store credit or cash for your well-preserved clothes. They will allow you to pick out the three garments you will not use and then exchange those with one piece that you will.

- Host a swap party for friends. Collect all the clothes you never wear anymore and keep them in a pile. Ask your friends to do that as well, then get together to trade your wares.

- Consider upcycling your old clothes. You can always look up crafts making videos on YouTube and teach yourself how to turn old t-shirts into dresses, bags, or shoes.

2. Organize your closet
   Simply follow these steps in making sure you have your closet situation in control:
   - General tips:
     - Keep in mind that if you can see a piece of clothing, then you will be more likely to want to wear it.
     - Make sure to use all of the available space in the closet, although you do have to keep everything organized.

- o Leave 1 or 2 hooks unused to make those quick-and-dirty cleanups easier.
- o Transfer out-of-season garments to another storage spot, such as underneath your bed.
- o Optimize the space available in high-up areas and behind deep shelves.

- Folded clothing:
    - o If you have a dresser, make sure to stack your garments vertically instead of horizontally so that they do not tumble and up cluttering your closet. Do this for your pajamas, socks, tights, and underwear.
    - o Avoid hanger bumps by folding all your knit pieces, such as sweaters, blouses, and T-shirts.
    - o Consider using extra shelving in shelves that you already have.
    - o If you have deep shelves, see to it that your clothes are folded properly. Make use of any remaining space at the back of folded clothes by storing your winter/summer sweaters and sandals back there.

- Hanging clothes:
    - Use matching hangers to help make all your organized clothes look nice.
    - A tiered hanger is a great tool for hanging skirts. If you would rather use a single skirt hanger, choose the ones that come with smooth rubber grips and spring clips.
    - Take advantage of cascading hooks. You can use 2 hooks at a time, and they work with almost all types of hanger.
    - Consider having another closet rod installed over the main one so that you will gain additional hanging space. Access the items you will keep up there with the help of a reaching rod or a stool.

- Bags:
    - Have your bags sit on a shelf instead of hanging them by the handles. This way, you effectively avoid getting the handles all stretched out.
    - Make sure to use a coat rack that you install over the closet door if you have to hang up your bags.
    - Remember to stuff tissue inside your bags in between use to help maintain their shape.

- Prevent your bags from slouching and losing their shape by using bookends.
- Try making a drawer from a long, old boot box to store your less-frequently-used bags in. Line the bags up inside, then slide into a deep shelf.

- Accessories:
  - Use screw-in hooks to hold your jewelry, belts, and sunglasses in place.
  - Use towel racks in hanging your scarves.
  - Keep smaller accessories organized inside jars, cups, and open boxes.

3. Stay true to your personal style as you put together outfits

- Stop following what style labels or seasonal trends dictate. Your minimalist wardrobe is something that is not only timeless, but also gives a glimpse of your true personality and allows you to be your most comfortable self. Start by asking yourself:

  - What message do I want what I wear to convey about me?

- - Which colors and patterns help me stay true to what I am?

  - What accessories best reflect my personality?

  - What fits and fabrics am I most at ease with wearing?

- Minimalist style is far from basic, especially when you adopt it with the help of elevated essentials – the foundation of your minimalist wardrobe. These good quality pieces are tastefully wearable and understatedly beautiful. They appear simple when talking about their colors or designs, but you get this vibe that there is something that sets them apart from other clothes. You will be able to figure out which clothes can be referred to as elevated basics by going with the following criteria:
  - Fabric: Even from a mile away, it would be easy to spot how well-made the fabric is in an elevated basic piece of clothing. It somehow gives out signs of luxury, but in an understated way.

- Quality: Price is not the only barometer of how well-made a garment is made. While expensive clothes usually come at a considerably higher price, you should still go to great lengths to find out if you are getting your money's worth. When looking at a piece of minimalist clothing, ask yourself whether great care has gone into making it, if it will last for years, if the fabric feels nice and natural on your skin, if the details are appropriate for its cut and fit, and if its silhouette complements your body shape.
- Fit/cut: It does not matter if an elevated basic item is slim-fit or slightly oversized, or if it is bought off-the-rack or is tailor-made for you, it will always look as if the garment was designed to fit you like a glove.
- Versatility: A minimalist wardrobe piece is something you can wear in a number of different ways. Even if you wear it time and time again, no one will be able to tell.
- Details: Elevated basics have their details nailed down. Whether it is a simple belt, an

edgy sleeve, or an asymmetric cut, the detail is interesting enough to guarantee a second look.

- Practice the art of layering that is central to the minimalist way of dressing. Layering your clothes allow you to be creative in how you put together an entire outfit while seeing to it that it does not steer away from practicality. Try your hand at minimalist layering with these tips:
    - Go monochrome: Take steps to vary the textures if you are going for a monochrome style. When you dress yourself in a single color (or different tones of the same color), the fastest way to turn your outfit from bland to wow is to use different fabrics and textures. Doing so adds dimension and depth to your outfit instead of looking wither too overwhelming or flat. Try combining softer and heavier textures such as cotton, wool, leather, and silk.
    - Knits on knits: Besides helping you look stylish, layering your knits also has a practical advantage. The key is to avoid using different pieces in the same heavy material; instead of

channeling the French's effortless way of dressing, you will end up looking frumpy. Consider mixing light with heavy knits; if the different pieces of your outfit are of the same light/heavy material, play with their colors and lengths to make sure the layers are distinct.

- White shirt galore: Take advantage of the white shirt's ability to work with practically any style of dressing or kind of outfit you want. Because it is neutral, you can wear with just about any other piece of clothing. You can wear it hanging loose, tucked in, under a sweater, over a dress, with a blazer, with a cardigan. You name it, the white shirt does it.
- Simply patterned: While the minimal style calls for simple patterns and neutral colors, it does not mean you cannot incorporate patterned items into your wardrobe. Go for just one subtle pattern that works with your outfit's color palette. It is guaranteed to make you look great, particularly if you wear it as your middle layer.

4. Look after your clothes
   It is important to see to it that you are washing and storing your clothes properly to enable you to wear them for many years to come.

   Here are tips on how to care for your clothes:

   - Do not wash too often. The more frequently you wash a piece of clothing, the more it will lose its quality.

   - Prevent any snagging and tangling in your clothes by closing their zippers and loosely tying their strings.

   - Take a closer look inside the collars. Stains from makeup, lotions, and other skin products easily accumulate in those parts. See to it that they are washed right away, particularly before you hang them inside the closet.

   - Hang your clothes in the bathroom and get them steamed while you shower, if you would rather not iron your clothes.

   - If possible, skip the dryer, as drying your cotton clothes repeatedly can result in cracks, weakened fibers, and pilling.

- When purchasing clothes, always choose those made of naturally durable fabrics that do not require that much care.

- Make sure to fold your clothes along their seams to help prevent unwanted creases from forming as well as keep their shape.

- Air out your clothes on hangers, preferably the wooden ones. See to it that the hanger's width does not exceed your shirt shoulders' width and that the shoulders are laid properly on the hanger. It helps to pull the fabric a little to reduce wrinkles and to make ironing easier. Make sure there is room between your ironed shirts when you store them in the closet after placing on hangers; this will help preserve their smoothness.

- Remember to check your clothes' pockets for coins, tissues, and other bits and pieces that can cause your laundry to become a big mess.

- Removing the odors from your denim jeans is as easy as either hanging them in the bathroom prior to a hot shower or freezing them inside a thick plastic bag within two days.

- Learn how to do basic repairs on clothes to help keep them around for longer as well as save you money.

5. Seeking help from the community
   You may be concerned that, in choosing to have a minimalist wardrobe, you may end up not having the right clothes to wear to special occasions. Admittedly, there are times when a person just needs to have an outfit (including wedding attire, vacation outfit, or maternity clothes) that he or she does not wear regularly. This is where online rental sites can help you – you can rent from them whatever it is you need to wear just once, which is an affordable and minimalist solution. You might also try swapping clothes with friends or neighbors who are also in the process of building their own minimalist wardrobes.

# Chapter 10 Mastering the Art of Minimalist Packing

Minimalist travelers love the idea of packing light because it helps them avoid being tied to the stuff they own, and enables them to do as much roaming about as they desire. Carrying a heavy bag is not only difficult and annoying, it can hold you back on your plans to travel. Getting through TSA becomes a much longer process then it should be, or finding adequate space in the overhead compartment to keep your bag safe during a flight, just because you are lugging around an unnecessarily hefty bag.

When you are able to free as much available space inside your luggage, you will find it easier to apply minimalism to your life as a whole and to let go of those bad habits you have acquired that end up making your life more cluttered. Practicing minimalism is something that needs you to shift your mindset, which you have to consistently work on. As a beginner in minimalist traveling, you might initially think that all you have to do is to bring less stuff the next time, when the reality is that you have to adopt an intentional lifestyle change involving plenty of planning and foresight.

To become a minimalist traveler, you need to dedicate much of your time and ability to identify which of your belongings are wants and which are needs. Doing so helps you become more open with regards to getting rid of unnecessary stuff and finally freeing up space for actually packing your things. You have to figure out:

•	What are the things you need to have with you on your trip?

•	Which items would you prefer to bring but that are not actually necessary?

•	What are the "just-in-case-but-will-never-get-used" belongings you plan to bring?

Packing Like A Minimalist

Getting your stuff together for a trip is as easy as following these steps:

1. Choose a smaller bag

Admittedly, picking out the travel luggage or backpack that suits you and your needs best will not be easy. But bringing yourself to pack with a smaller bag actually forces you to make do with that bag and give your best shot at putting all of your stuff in there, which is an effective way to dip your toes into the art of minimalist packing. By working with a small bag, you are setting yourself in the right direction towards travelling minimally.

Paring down the number of items you have to bring on a trip becomes easier if you do not give yourself any additional space in your bag for packing non-essentials, especially those that will not get used at all. You will find it more convenient and practical to just go with a carry-on luggage, as this allows you to just stick your bag beneath the seat in your front instead of having to find an overhead storage bin space in your flight. When choosing the best bag to pack with, keep in mind that the ideal bag is one that lets you compartmentalize the items in your packing list to help keep everything accessible and clutter-free, such as a daypack, a crossbody duffel bag, or a travel backpack.

2. Bring only the essentials

Once you are done with picking the right bag to pack your things in, the next step would be to evaluate everything written down on your packing list. Regardless of whether you are packing for a short trip or a long-term travel, it is during this step that you will be able to identify what your necessities are and what items are unnecessary and are best left at home.

- To help you pinpoint the items you need to include in your packing list, try asking yourself the following?

  - What items bring me the most comfort and joy?

  - What habits do I currently have that I can temporarily remove from my usual routine? (wearing jewelry, applying contour makeup, etc.)

  - Will this item be too heavy for me to carry?

  - Could I bring a travel-sized version of this essential item?

  - How often will I truly be able to use this particular item while I am traveling?

- You might ask yourself exactly which essential items should you be bringing with you. You need to make sure you will carry your ID, passport, credit cards, and cash with you on the trip. It is also important that you remember to bring your phone, headphones, and charger to help you stay connected with family and friends while you are traveling, to record your memorable experiences in photos and videos, and to keep boredom at bay during down time.

- You would also need your bag or luggage to carry other essentials like a toothbrush, a water bottle, your prescription medications, a light jacket, and comfortable walking shoes. You will need these basics while traveling; all other essentials like toothpaste, shampoo, and soap can then be bought at your destination.

3. Put together your capsule wardrobe

You need to have a capsule wardrobe if you tend to over-pack clothes. Your capsule wardrobe will include several items of clothing that you can mix and match. This helps you make the most of your bag's space while letting you get dressed each morning in the shortest amount of time. When you have already figured out that each of your selected pieces go well together, putting together an outfit suddenly becomes an effortless task.

- Make sure the capsule wardrobe you create includes items from these categories: layers, outerwear, lounge, workout, formal attire, and accessories. Consider your lifestyle or the type of travel you will be taking in adjusting these categories. Keeping that in mind, gather all the clothing pieces you will use for every category, and then pare it down. Think about how useful each piece will be, how well each item fits you, and whether each piece matches the other ones included in your capsule wardrobe.

- Select nine tops, five pants, and three to four pairs of shoes. Constantly aim to pick even fewer items than this, based on the duration of your trip and the categories you have to include according the season.

4. Manage your toiletries

How you limit your toiletries for travel is really all up to your preferences.

- For some, going on a minimalist trip might mean bringing just a toothbrush and nothing else. Others may prefer to carry along mini-versions of each cream, solution, or tool they will need.

- The important thing is that you will be able to tuck away all of your toiletries into a small pouch that you can easily reach for whenever you need it.

- Keep in mind that, as a rule, you may not need every cleanser and every lip balm you usually use on a daily basis. Try eliminating any unnecessary item you may have included in your toiletries list. For sure, there is no way you could be wearing a handful of hair gel, full-on makeup, or strappy heels during your trip. See to it that you identify which habits and products are worth leaving at home.

5. Shoes and other accessories

The types of shoes and other accessories you will need to bring while traveling will depend on the type of activities you plan on doing during the trip and the season of your destination.

- Remember that for any trip, it is a must that you are able to lounge comfortably, so make sure to pack a pair of your favorite sandals, flip flops, or another type of open-toed footwear. If you plan on exploring the globe, once city at a time, you may be better off bringing your well-worn walking shoes. If you anticipate the idea of going for a nice night out in the new destination, you might want to include a pair of fancy heels or boots.

- If you have to bring along accessories, strive to keep the number of items low. Consider including a hat, a pair of sunglasses, or some minimal jewelry in your list of accessories to wear while traveling. You can also add a scarf, a journal, and ear plugs. What you deem is an essential accessory is up to you, but make sure to pick wisely in order to avoid clutter in your luggage or bag.

6. Quit trying to completely fill your bag

While it is wise to make use of every space and corner inside your bag, it does not make sense to try filling it completely, as this can result in over-packing. Stay true to your minimalist ways by letting the following space-maximizing strategies help you pack smartly:

- Instead of placing your bulkiest item in your bag, wear it while traveling to avoid adding to the weight you have to carry.

- Stuff your underwear and socks into your hat to save space as well as help the hat retain its shape.

- Prevent your jewelry from getting tangled by storing them inside a pill case.

- Make sure your shirts' collars stay stiff by wrapping belts in them.

- To help keep clothing items smell fresh when unpacking, toss in a few dryer sheets.

- Roll your clothes.
- Take advantage of packing cubes.
- Stuff underwear and socks inside your shoes before putting them in your bag's bottom compartment.
- Keep your small cords organized by stashing them inside your sunglasses case.

1. Try this minimalist packing list

    You will find this list works perfectly for both men and women, for any occasion, in any climate, and in any destination.

Essential items:

- Cash or credit cards
- Clothing
- Water bottle
- ID/passport
- Long-sleeved shirt (1)
- T-shirts (3)
- Tank top (1)
- Button-down shirt or blouse (1)
- Dress or another attire for special occasion (1)
- Light jacket (1)
- Pair of pants (1)

- Pair of shorts (1)
- Pair of leggings (1)
- Bra (1) + sports bra (1)
- Pair of underwear (6)
- Pairs of socks (3 to 6)
- Pair of underwear (6)
- Windbreaker (1)
- Packable down jacket (1)
- Swim trunks/bathing suit (1)

<u>Toiletries (mini-sized):</u>

- Toothpaste/toothbrush
- Razor
- Comb/hairbrush
- Deodorant
- Soap
- Sunscreen
- Moisturizer
- ChapStick
- Hand sanitizer
- Tweezers
- Nail clippers
- First aid kit – including band aids

2. Consider these additional minimalist packing tricks

- Consider investing in a well-organized travel bag: Minimalism may be all about steering away from accumulating more and more stuff as a way of feeling fulfilled with your life, but there are items that are worth spending your money on. This includes a well-organized travel bag that you can use for years to come. Choose one that is ergonomically designed and comes with lots of pockets as well as versatility features. You might consider purchasing a reliable travel bag that you can convert into a backpack and is paired with a detachable daypack. Traveling minimally becomes easier when your clothes, toiletries, and electronics are separated and organized beautifully inside your travel bag.

- Plan on doing some laundry: If you are planning on taking a trip that lasts for a week or longer, you cannot possibly claim to be taking minimalism seriously by wearing the same outfit every day. Take advantage of Laundromats, which exist in many towns and cities. Another way you could be minimal in your approach to doing the laundry is to hand-wash your worn clothes in the tub or sink.

- Purchase your groceries on the go: Dining out each meal can wreak havoc on your aim to travel minimally if you are either watching your diet or are traveling on a limited budget. Eat healthier and save money at the same time by going to local fresh markets and grocery stores to buy your food while traveling. Seek out hotels and hostels equipped with a kitchen area so that you are able to cook at least one meal each day. It also helps to carry with you some re-sealable bags or plastic storage containers filled with snacks and meals that you can eat later. You can bring along a water bottle to help you avoid becoming dehydrated for the duration of your trip (except when you are not sure whether or not the tap water in your travel destination is safe for drinking). Remember that practicing minimalism is not just about getting rid of and preventing clutter; it also involves reducing the amount of waste you create and release to the environment.

- Ship back any souvenirs: For many individuals, shopping for souvenirs is naturally a part of the entire travel experience. And even minimalists tend to remember the trips they have taken by making sure to collect as well as give mementos. Rather than purchasing big, heavy souvenirs, go for the ones that are easy to carry, like patches, magnets, ornaments, and jewelry. If something interesting in a souvenir shop catches your eye, ask if you can have them ship the item for you. You might also try going to the local post office, then arrange for a box filled with some souvenirs to be shipped back home. This way, you do away with carrying them around as well as constantly being worried about breaking them.

- Simplify your wallet: Prior to leaving for your trip, remember to declutter your wallet. Clear out any cards, receipts, and other unnecessary items and fill it only with the cash and credit card you need.

# Chapter 11 Saving the Environment by Living Minimally

Far from being overwhelming and impractical, living minimally is essentially about living your life intentionally and taking into consideration the impact of your actions. In this regard, by practicing minimalism, you take steps to reduce your eco-footprint and see to it that the environment is not stripped bare by overconsumption.

Help protect the environment by incorporating minimalism into your life with these tips:

1. Stop using disposable containers.
   That single-use plastic container used to hold your lunch is one of the easiest things you can give up that has a direct impact on the environment. All over the world, people are pushing the message of saying no to the use of plastic straws, but then the act of buying that stainless steel straw is one step only. Keep in mind that you can contribute three to four plastic bags to the world's big garbage disposal problem from a single takeaway meal alone. You can use a tiffin carrier to avoid

this issue, foregoing the plastic spoon and fork that it automatically comes with, and press on with the resolve to walk away without throwing out anything. It also helps to no longer order your food from deliveries to avoid the large quantities of waste it inevitably comes with. Try making your own simple meals within the comfort of your home. If you are out of the house, bring a food box with you, and always have your reusable cutlery on standby for those times when you have to deal with takeaways. Although people usually disposable plastic because of how convenient it is, take the high road and view the situation as your way of preventing more chemicals in plastic from getting into your food.

2. Grow your own vegetables
   Another way you could live the minimalist way and saving the environment at the same time is by growing your own food at home. While reducing your carbon footprint, you are also making sure that what you eat is free from pesticides and other chemicals. You can easily grow your own veggies in a small space in your yard.

   - Try planting edible plants that do not require a lot in terms of maintenance, such as cherry tomatoes, long beans, mint, and Brazilian spinach.

- If it is your first time with gardening, and you do not really have that much space, rest assured that you can grow plants in pots. You can take baby steps with peppers and cherry tomatoes at the back door, and some salad greens or a mini herb garden on the kitchen windowsill.

- Get started with growing food at home with these tips:

    o Peppers: You can grow spicy jalapenos and tangy bell peppers in compact plant containers to keep them from getting too big. Make sure to place the pots in a warm spot outside where they get exposed to sunlight. Remember to water your pepper plants lots of water. If you choose to grow them in pots inside the house, see to it that you use supplemental lighting to ensure their proper growth.

    o Tomatoes: If you are tight on garden space, consider growing your tomato plants in pots. You can choose a tomato variety that grows well in containers. Make sure to always water your tomato plants and to place them in a spot where they will get lots of sunlight.

- Microgreens: Microgreens refer to mustard greens, beet greens, collard greens, and other tender plant shoots. Instead of buying them at stores, where they could be pricy, grown your own on a windowsill.

- Scallions: Maybe you are always purchasing scallions and regrettably letting them go bad. Try cutting off the white parts of the scallions the next time you purchase them. After securing with rubber bands, put inside a glass filled with ½-inch of water. Replace the water every day and within seven to ten days, you will have grown yourself new scallion shoots, with their roots becoming twice as long. Plant in your container, then snip the green parts as needed.

- Salad greens: Salad greens are easy to grow in pots or other containers placed on a porch or another outdoor space. Snip the plants above their roots as much as you need, as they will just keep on growing.

- Mushrooms: You can grow your own specialty mushrooms by using a mushroom kit that allows you to grow them in an indoor box. Simply open the box before placing on your windowsill. Mist the growing medium (recycled coffee grounds) regularly and, on your first harvest, you will have yielded two pounds' worth of mushrooms within ten days.

3. Get your household solutions refilled the BYOB way
   Like many people, a large number of your regular cleaning essentials are likely sold in plastic bottles. You need the contents, not the plastic bottles they come in, but you actually for the latter. Have your containers of grooming necessities refilled

at refill centers instead of buying them the usual way.

4. Make compost at home

People somehow mistake organic waste to be better compared to inorganic waste, reasoning that the former decomposes by natural means. But when organic waste lands in a landfill, it decomposes by anaerobic activity that produces the harmful greenhouse gas called methane. Instead of letting your organic waste reach its way to landfills and contribute to the greenhouse effect, consider composting at home. Starting a compost pile is easy to do in three steps:

- Purchase a container
Get a large ceramic or plastic one at department stores or gardening shops. Create spaces for ventilation and water drainage by poking holes in your container's lid and base, then add a tray beneath it for catching the drainage. Make sure to keep your compost pile somewhere cool and exposed to lots of sunlight.

- Prep your composting bin

See to it that you prep the composting bin before tossing scrapped food in it. Begin by cutting out paper strips from old newspapers. Soak the strips of paper in water before using half of those strips in lining the bottom part of your compost bin. Cover with soil and drop in worms, the number of which will depend on the size of the bin (you will need one pound of worms for each square foot area).

- Add your food scraps
  Once you are done with the paper-soil-worms part, start tossing in the food scraps you have collected. Your compost pile can in consist of tea, coffee, vegetables, fruits, egg shells, leaves, produce peels, tea bags, coffee filters, and paper.

  - Never add meat, bones, citrus, dairy, animal waste, or anything made of plastic.

  - Remember to always cover your compost pile with more soaked paper strips whenever you add scraps to it.

  - You can keep adding scraps to your compost pile. Try having 2 compost bins in your home so you could alternate between them. This way, you give the worms the time they need to decompose the food scraps, and you also get more space when you use that bin the next time. As soon as the compost bin is full and its contents have decomposed, you can transfer the contents outside and use it for gardening.

5. Be minimalist and eco-friendly with your personal grooming supplies

If you look inside your bathroom's trash can, you will likely discover items like plastic wrappers, empty toothpaste tubes, cotton balls, and empty shampoo bottles. These items are also likely to end up in landfills, adding more to the already huge amount of trash created by wasteful plastic packaging and causing plastic pollution. In one month alone, you can only imagine how much plastic waste your bathroom habits can cause you to generate.
Say goodbye to using one-use disposable items from now on and give the following minimalist bathroom products a try:

- Replace cotton swabs with reusable facial rounds or cloths. You can only use a large number of commercial cotton swabs once, and to make matters worse, you have to deal with the fact that plastic is used to package them. To stay true to your mission to save the environment by living minimally, consider replacing your regular cotton swabs with reusable facial rounds. You can reuse them as frequently as you want, as you could just throw them in the washer as soon as they get filthy. As an alternative, you might also try using cleansing cloths that can be washed and reused after using them to remove dirt, oil, and makeup from your face.

- Use a shampoo bar instead of bottled shampoo. A shampoo bar is more minimalist and environment-friendly than your conventional shampoo because it lasts way longer and does not come in a plastic bottle.

- Instead of using regular conditioner, which also comes in plastic bottles, try using apple cider vinegar that has been mixed with several drops of your favorite essential oil, such as tea tree oil. This homemade hair conditioner will help remove residue that has accumulated in your strands, treat dandruff, and maintain your hair's softness.

- Avoid buying regular toothpaste that comes in non-recyclable plastic tubes. Consider switching to toothpaste powders or an all-natural toothpaste brand that is packaged in a glass jar.

- A minimalist and environment-friendly substitute for disposable and plastic razors are safety razors, which have blades that are made with a stainless steel material. These razors last a lifetime and their blades can be recycled.

- Not only is your conventional dental floss made from nylon, it is also spooled around a plastic container. Try the compostable silk dental floss alternative that comes inside a refillable glass container.

- Stop buying tissue paper that comes packaged in plastic wrapping. Instead, choose brands that come inside cardboard boxes and that you can purchase at office supply stores or through the Internet.

- Rather than using Q-tips that come with plastic stems, go for those that come with wood applicators, which make them compostable.

- Choose wooden combs and brushes over those that are made of plastic.

- Make the minimalist switch from plastic nail brushes to wood nail brushes that have natural bristles.

- Tampons are made with fibers, chemicals, and bleach that can remain inside the body. Try reusable menstrual cups that are healthier for the body, effectively provide leakage protection, and environment-friendly.

- Replace the trash can you have sitting in your bathroom with a compost bucket. This way, you can actually compost your used tissue, hair strands, and nail clippings.

6. Try going meatless

Going minimalist means engaging in practices that bring the most meaning and value to your life. One way you can practice this philosophy is by deciding not to eat meat. This helps to simplify your diet and cooking habits, and also allows you to reduce your eco-footprint. Heed these tips on how to go meatless the minimalist way:

- Consider going meatless for a week before starting your eat-no-meat plan. You can have a simple veggie burger with salad for lunch.

- Begin by using beans as a protein source in your favorite meals in place of poultry or meat. Using familiar recipes that make use of no-meat ingredients is the easiest route to changing into a more minimalist way of eating. You can make these substitutions in recipes that have marinara sauce, sweet and sour sauce, or other strong flavors. You can then play with plant-based meat substitutes once you get the hang of incorporating more beans into your diet.

- At grocery stores, sample different kinds of vegetarian convenience foods, choose one that you enjoy eating, and purchase it. Make sure it offers a nutritional boost by providing extra nutrients. Pick soy products that have been fortified with vitamin B12, vitamin D, and calcium. Give soy crumbles and tofu a try and enjoy their mild flavors and ability to absorb the seasonings in whatever recipe.

# Conclusion

I'd like to thank you and congratulate you for transiting my lines from start to finish.
I hope this book was able to help you see that it is possible to live simply and contentedly, that you do not need to accumulate one material thing after another in order to achieve happiness in life.
The next step is to learn to embrace minimalism in your daily life and to regularly declutter the different aspects of your lifestyle.
I wish you the best of luck!

www.ingramcontent.com/pod-product-compliance
Lightning Source LLC
Chambersburg PA
CBHW070103120526
44588CB00034B/2014